DIARY OF THOMAS BELLINGHAM.

COLONEL THOMAS BELLINGHAM.

Copied from a painting by Gervas, in the collection at Castle Bellingham.

ABIGAIL, WIFE OF COLONEL BELLINGHAM.

From a painting in the collection at Castle Bellingham.

SOCIAL LIFE AND NATIONAL MOVEMENTS
IN THE 17TH CENTURY.
(1688-89-90).

DIARY

OF

THOMAS BELLINGHAM,

An Officer under William III.

COMPLETE TRANSCRIPT AND NOTES

BY

ANTHONY HEWITSON,

*Author of " History of Preston," " Stonyhurst College—Present and Past,"
" Churches and Chapels" (Preston and District), " Northward," &c.,
and Joint-Editor of the " Tyldesley Diary."*

INTRODUCTION BY

A. R. MADDISON, F.S.A.,

Canon of Lincoln Cathedral and Rector of Burton-by-Lincoln.

WITH ILLUSTRATIONS, &c.

The Naval & Military Press Ltd

in association with

The National Army Museum, London

Published jointly by

The Naval & Military Press Ltd

Unit 10 Ridgewood Industrial Park,
Uckfield, East Sussex,
TN22 5QE England

Tel: +44 (0) 1825 749494
Fax: +44 (0) 1825 765701

www.naval-military-press.com
www.military-genealogy.com
www.militarymaproom.com

and

The National Army Museum, London

www.national-army-museum.ac.uk

INTRODUCTION.

The writer of this diary was one of a cadet branch of a family which took its name from Bellingham, a small market town in Northumberland, about 16 miles N N.W. of Hexham. Here the Bellinghams were lords of the manor from a very early period, and down to the latter part of the 17th century manorial quit rents were paid to them after the actual estates had passed into other hands. In 1715 these were held by the ill-fated Earl of Derwentwater, on whose attainder and execution they passed, by grant of the Crown, to Greenwich Hospital.

It is a striking instance of the tenacity of local tradition that Capt. Alan Bellingham, a descendant of the diarist, was welcomed, in 1807, by the inhabitants of Bellingham as one of the old race. He records in a journal in that year that in visiting Bellingham he was " constantly addressed by the title ' Lord,' as they declared I was the rightful Lord of the Manor there." He attended the Court of the Manor at Wark, where the inhabitants of Bellingham did suit and service, and says, " Upon the Heir of the last Alan Bellingham being called in Court, I immediately answered, and claimed the Manor and Royalties attached to Bellingham. Great civility and attention was shown me by Mr. Peters (the solicitor), who holds the Court for Greenwich Hospital, and by Mr. Walton, the principal Receiver. I was invited to dine at the Court Dinner."

What made the Bellinghams leave Northumberland, for Westmorland, was the marriage of a Richard Bellingham with Christian, or Margaret, daughter and heiress of Sir Gilbert de Burneshide or Burneshead, Knt., by which they acquired the lordship of Burneshead Hall, near Kendal, in the latter county, early in the 14th century. Very possibly they were not sorry to leave so unsettled and lawless a region as Tynedale, exposed to constant depredations from the Scots, for more peaceful quarters. At any rate, from that marriage they were Bellinghams of Burneshead Hall.

In the 15th century the family divided into several branches. Sir Robert Bellingham, the then head of the family, had a large family of sons. Of these Sir Henry Bellingham succeeded him at Burneshead, took the side of Lancaster in the Wars of the Roses, and was knighted by Lord Clifford, at the battle of Wakefield, 31st March, 1460. But a reverse speedily followed, and on the 10th of February, 1462-3, his estates being forfeited were granted by Edward IV. to Sir William Parr, Knt., and his brother John. Fortune, however, again smiled on the family under the Red Rose, and Sir Roger Bellingham, his son, was made a Knight Banneret at the battle of Stoke, in 1487, while Sir Roger's son Robert distinguished himself by capturing Lambert Simnel at the same battle, for which he, too, was knighted. He, however, had only daughters, and through them most of the estates passed from the family. Burneshead he sold to Sir Thomas Clifford, Knt. Two branches were planted by Richard and Thomas Bellingham, younger brothers of the above Sir Henry, in Lincolnshire and Sussex respectively. The Lincolnshire line ended, so far as its connection with that county was concerned, in Richard Bellingham, the Governor of Massachusetts in the 17th century. The Sussex line was exceedingly prolific, and divided into branches at Erringham (from which came Sir Edward Bellingham, Lord Deputy of Ireland, temp. Hen. VIII.), Hangleton, Lyminster, and Newtimber. These were all flourishing early in the 17th century, but gradually decayed and became extinct. The most vigorous offshoot from the main stem was that which was planted by Alan Bellingham, the eighth son, and youngest brother of Sir Henry above mentioned. He, according to the Heraldic Visitations and the County History of Westmorland, was Treasurer of Berwick and Deputy Warden of the Marches, and the more modern motto of the family, " Amicus amico," is taken from the distich which commemorates him—

> " Amicus amico Alanus,
> Belliger belligero Bellinghamus."

He was living in the reigns of Henry VI. and Henry VII., and is considered by genealogical authorities to have acquired the very extensive estates at Levens, Helsington (Westmorland), and elsewhere which were enjoyed by his descendants. It is highly probable, however, that there has been some confusion between him and his grandson, also called Alan, who died in 1577, and who can be shown by documentary evidence to have made large purchases of land, and to have been Treasurer of Berwick. He was appointed to that office by Writ of Privy Seal, 2nd August, 1557, with a salary of £20 per annum. By his second wife,

Dorothy Sandford, whom he must have married rather late in life, he left a very large family, of which the sons were all under age at his death. The eldest, Thomas Bellingham, died only three years after his father, unmarried. The second, James, carried on the line at Levens. One of the younger sons, Robert, was admitted into the Middle Temple on the 2nd of August, 1595. He was the ancestor of the writer of this diary. The eldest son, James, was Knighted in 1603. He practically rebuilt Levens Hall, and fitted up the rooms with the beautiful wainscotting which is so well known, and has been so well described. The fortunes of the family attained their zenith in his life-time. He declined a Baronetcy, which was thereupon conferred on his eldest son, Henry, in 1620. In 1642 Sir James died, and trouble quickly came with the miseries of Civil War.

In 1646 Sir Henry had to reckon with the victorious Parliament. His "Delinquency" was that being a member of the Long Parliament he deserted it, and went to Oxford and sat in the Assembly there. He acknowledged this to be true, but pleaded, in extenuation of his fault, "that he took the National Covenant in his parish church in the country, before William Curwen, minister, the 12 Sept., 1645, as by his certificate doth appear. He hath also taken the negative oath the 30 June, 1646." The Parliament, however, being greatly in need of money, was not disposed to show much mercy to an unfortunate Royalist, and Sir Henry was ordered to furnish a schedule of his estates and the rental. His fine was fixed at £3,228. It is interesting to note in the schedule the following:—"He is seized of an estate to him and his heirs of and in the Lordship of Bellingham, in the Co. of Northumberland, of the yearly value before these troubles of £5." This so-called rental was really the quit rents paid to him as Lord of the Manor, while the bulk of the estate had gone into other hands. But Sir Henry's troubles were not yet over. A petition from him to the "Commissioners for Compounding with Delinquents," dated 27th November, 1648, states that "This last summer Sir Marmaduke Langdale coming with his forces into Westmorland, and the petitioner's estate lyeing under his Command, and being daily threatened to be plundered, and seeing no visible forces to protect him, He was againe drawne to ingage against the Parliament, not out of disaffection to them but meerly to preserve himselfe from ruyne, for which he is again sequestred." For this act of self-defence he was fined £1,971. The son has now to share in the punishment inflicted on the father, and on the 4th of May, 1649, the humble petition of "James Bellingham, Esq., sonne and heire of Sir Henry Bellingham, Knt. and Bart.," was presented to the Commissioners for Composition. He, too, confessed to having been a " member of the honorable House of Commons, and having deserted the Parliament, and having been in arms against the Parliament in the late engagement." His separate estate, independent of that settled by Sir Henry on him and his wife, was but small, and his fine was only £200. But the family troubles were not yet over: they culminated in 1650, when Sir Henry and his only son James died, within a few days of one another, at Levens Hall. It is sad to think that Sir Henry's last days were embittered by fresh trouble. A certain John Musgrave had given information to the Commissioners for Compounding that Sir Henry in giving in a schedule of his estates and rental had greatly under-valued the amount of the latter and concealed a good deal of his property. In the beginning of June, 1650, Sir Henry went to the Commissioners, at Kendal, and engaged " to make satisfaction for any under-values that might afterwards appear, etc., and caused a horse to be provided for the journey, intending to send up to London or Newcastle; which of the two being the proper place for him to compound. But that in the meantime it pleased God to visit him with sickness, whereon he died." The precise date of his death is not known, but it must have ben very shortly after making his will, which is dated 15th of October, 1650. He made his son James sole executor, who must have been lying sick unto death at the time, for he left a nuncupative will which, with his father's, was proved by his relict Katharine on the 24th of May, 1651, when the administration was granted to her. The will clearly shows that the son had survived the father, though only for a few days, as he is styled "Sir James Bellingham, Baronet," and his widow " the Lady Katharine Bellingham."

The Commissioners for Compounding, in a letter dated 26th October, 1650, distinctly state that Sir Henry Bellingham was then dead, and in a postscript add, " Since the writing of the lettre above said we have received certaine information that Sir James Bellingham is *this present evening* deceased, neither he nor his father having left any issue male, and when we knowe upon whome the state descends we shall certifie, etc." Between the 15th of October and the evening of the 26th Sir Henry and Sir James had both passed away. The heir male was Sir Henry's brother, Alan Bellingham, to whom his father, the elder Sir James, had given the estate of Gathorne, in Westmorland, on his marriage with Susan, daughter of Marmaduke Constable, of Wassand, in Co. York. Alan, who at the Heraldic Visitation of Westmorland, in 1664, gave his age at 68, now petitions the Commissioners, 21st November, 1650, and after stating that Sir Henry Bellingham, Bart., of Levens, and his only son, Sir James, "both being delinquents, are very lately and suddenly dead, together with the *grandchild* the only heir of that line of the family being but above half a year old," etc.: "He prays the rather because he has been no delinquent, but ever faithful to the Parliament," etc., that he may have time to establish his succession to the estates. Certainly it would be natural to suppose that a faithful adherent to the cause of the Parliament would escape sequestration; but, unfortunately, the Parliament wanted money, and Sir Henry's under-valuation of his estates had not been atoned for. Alan accordingly found himself obliged to pay, 24th Feb., 1651-2, the sum of £1,413 12s. od. for the "under-values"; Lady Katharine, Sir James' widow, had to pay £620 19s. od.; and Sir Henry's daughters and co-heirs, Agnes wife of Thomas Wentworth and Elizabeth wife of John Lowther, were duly mulcted according to their portions.

Alan Bellingham carried on the family line at Levens. He lived to old age, and seems to have been prudent in the management of his affairs, for he was able to leave the manor of Whitwell, in Co. York, to his second son, Henry Bellingham, who in all the Baronetages is put down as ancestor of the Irish branch of the family. But, so far from this being the case, he had an only daughter and heiress, Frances, who married Sir Reginald Graham, Bart., of Norton Conyers. Alan left to his third son, Thomas Bellingham, his property at Houghton, in Co. Durham. He died unmarried. In 1672 Alan died, and his eldest son, James Bellingham, succeeded him. He married three times. By his first wife he had a daughter, Elizabeth, who married Timothy Mauleverer, of Arncliffe, Co. York. By his second wife he had three sons, Alan, Henry, and William; and five daughters: Mary, wife of Alexander Johnson, of Preston, Co. Lancaster; Agnes, wife of William Patten, of Preston; Bridget, wife of Timothy Fetherstonhaugh, of Kirkoswald, Cumberland; Elizabeth, wife of John Seahouse, of Seascale, Cumberland; and Dorothy, who died unmarried. James Bellingham died in 1680.

The period is now reached when the writer of the diary comes on the scene, and it will be well to give his descent. We must go back to Alan Bellingham, of Levens, who died in 1577. His brass, in Kendal Parish Church, says that he had vii. sons and viii. daughters, and that v. sons and vii. daughters survived him. He is said to have been 61 years of age at his death, 7 May, 1577. His post-mortem Inquisition gives, as is usual, a considerable portion of his will, which was dated 15th of June, 1568—nine years previous to his death. Clearly several of his sons were born afterwards, for he only mentions three at first—Thomas, James, and Henry; entailing the estates on them and their male issue; failing that, on his nephew, Thomas Bellingham, son of his deceased brother James. It is noteworthy that the manor of Levens was then held in jointure by Mrs. Preston, formerly wife of Richard Redman, the original possessor of the estate, for the term of her life; so that it could hardly have been purchased by Alan's grandfather, Alan, who is said in all printed accounts of the family to have bought it. Evidently Alan, in making his will, in 1568, left vacant spaces for the insertion of future sons, as he goes on to say that in the event of his third son, Henry, dying without male issue, the lands are to go to his next son, "yf yt please God to send one (wch is now my sonne Alan Bellingham)." Then he says, "and to my next sonne, yf God send another, I give and bequeth my manors, lands, and tenements in Great Strickland, and Melkinthorpe, etc." This son was Robert, the ancestor of the Irish branch, who, as has been already told, entered the Middle Temple on the 2nd of August, 1595, his elder brother Alan having been admitted on the 25th of April, 1588. What led to his going to Ireland must be to some extent conjecture; but it is worthy of note that his sister, Grace Bellingham, had married for her second husband Gerard Lowther, Lord Chief Justice of the C.P. in Ireland. Robert Bellingham had good reason for practising in the Irish law courts with such a connection; and in 1611 we find him High Sheriff of Co. Longford. Between 1616 and 1620 he was Attorney to the Second Remembrancer of the Exchequer. In 1620 James I. granted to him "dilectum et fidelem subditum nostrum Robertum Bellingham, generosum," the wardship of Dominic Trant, gent., of Dingletush, Co. Kerry. In 1626 he petitions to be restored "to the counties which were withholden from him by one Warren," in connection with his office of Attorney of the Second Remembrancer. In 1639 he seems to have revisited his English home, as he was buried at Kendal in that year. He had married Margaret Whyte, of the family of Whyte of Clongill, Co. Meath, who survived him and was buried, 13th November, 1668, at St. Werburgh's, Dublin. By her he had two sons and a daughter—Daniel, Henry, and Jane.

Daniel was born about 1620; was sworn of the Goldsmiths' Guild in 1644; was Sheriff of Dublin, 1655; Alderman, 1656; and Lord Mayor of Dublin, 1665-6. He was Major of the City Militia in 1659; was Knighted, 1662; and was created a Baronet on the 18th of March, 1666-7. He married, about 1645, Jane, daughter of Richard Barlow, of Cheshire, who survived him. He died in 1672, and was buried in St. Werburgh's Church with his mother. He was succeeded by his only son, Sir Richard Bellingham, of Dubber Castle, who was baptised 21st October, 1648, at St. Werburgh's, and admitted to Lincoln's

Inn, 15th of September, 1670. He died unmarried, and was buried at St. Werburgh's, in June, 1699, when the Baronetcy became extinct, and his property passed to his sisters.

Henry Bellingham, Sir Daniel's brother, was also a citizen and goldsmith of Dublin. He married Lucy, daughter of William Sibthorpe, of Dunany, Co. Louth, niece of Sir Christopher Sibthorpe, Knt., Lord Chief Justice of the K.B., and of Robert Sibthorpe, Bishop of Kilfenora. In the troublous times Henry entered the army, and while his kinsmen, in Westmorland, were being sequestered and fined for being Royalists, he was cornet of a troop in Hewson's regiment of horse. In 1654 he was High Sheriff of Co. Kildare. As he was the first possessor of the estate now called Castle Bellingham, it will be well to state how he acquired it. The original name was Gernonstown, and no doubt belonged to the Gernons, a Norman family, very early settled in Ireland. It was not an uncommon practice to give grants of land that had been forfeited during the Rebellion of 1641, in Ireland, to officers and soldiers in lieu of pay, which was often much in arrears. The Golden Vale, in Tipperary, is an example in point, having been largely parcelled out among Cromwellian soldiers. Colonel John Hewson's regiment of cavalry had been disbanded, and Henry Bellingham no doubt had money owing to him. A document dated 25th of May, 1654, states that John Perryn, of Dublin, late a trooper in Col. Hewson's regiment, had had 13 acres in Kilsaran (the parish in which Gernonstown was a township) granted to him, in lieu of £38 due to him from the Commonwealth, for services done in Ireland; and he sold this to Henry Bellingham, late a cornet in the same regiment. Another document states that certain lands and tenements had been granted to Henry Bellingham for his services in the late war, and that he was in actual possession of them on the 7th of May, 1659. These consisted of 619 acres in Gernonstown, 183 acres in Milestown, 80 acres in Williamstown, 108 acres in Lynne, and 86 acres in Adamstown; amounting to 1,077 acres of Plantation measure, 1,744 acres of English measure. These were all confirmed to him, 24th of April, 1666. He is styled " Captain " in this document. Little is known about him beyond what has been stated. If he was an officer in the Cromwellian army, he was a Royalist at the Restoration, and represented Co. Louth in Parliament, 1661. He was High Sheriff in 1671. The sister of Sir Daniel and Capt. Henry Bellingham was Jane, who married Sir George Gilbert, Alderman of Dublin, who was Knighted by the Duke of Ormond on the same day as his brother-in-law, Sir Daniel Bellingham.

It would be interesting to know more about the early life of the writer of
the diary, Thomas Bellingham, who, with a sister Anne, was the only son of
Capt. Henry.   All that is known is that he was born about 1646, and in 1671
married Abigail, daughter of William Handcock, of Twyford, in Co. Westmeath.
His sister Anne married Robert Bickerton, of Cantiluff, in Co. Armagh, whose
sister Jane was the second wife of Henry, sixth Duke of Norfolk.   Throughout
the diary the Colonel frequently alludes to cousins—those on the Bellingham
side in Westmorland, and those who were related to him through his uncle,
Sir Daniel Bellingham, and his sister, Mrs. Bickerton.   In spite of his father
having been on the opposite side, during the Civil War, his Bellingham cousins
seem to have warmly welcomed him.   Who these were it is necessary now to
say.   James Bellingham, of Levens, who died in 1680, left a large family,
already mentioned.   Alan, the eldest, was destined to ruin the estate and die
in exile.   Henry, the second son, died unmarried in 1687, leaving what he
had to leave to his brother Alan.   William, the third son, was a barrister, and
had he been the eldest things would have been very different.   Of the
married daughters, Mrs. Johnson and Mrs. Patten seem to have come most in
contact with Col. Bellingham.   He mentions them frequently in the diary,
along with their brother, William Bellingham.   He never, however, mentions
the unhappy spendthrift who, at the very time the diary commences (1 Aug.,
1688) must have been deeply involved, nor is there any allusion to Levens
Hall being shut up when the owner had fled to France.   Tradition, as often
happens in such cases, has left a suspicion of foul play with regard to the
eventual sale of Levens; but the documentary evidence does not support it.
Alan Bellingham made his will on the 12th of October, 1688, before he left
England, and makes over his estates to trustees to sell and pay his debts.
Among these is one of £13,000 owing to Richard Graham, Esq.   He leaves
£50 apiece for mourning to his sisters, whom he names Mauleverer, Johnson,
Patten,   Fetherstone   (i.e.,   Fetherstonhaugh),   Senhouse,   and   Dorothy
Bellingham.   He bequeaths a "Bay Horse called Madcapp unto Mr. Edward
Ridley"; and all the residue, after payment of debts, to his brother, William
Bellingham, whom he makes executor, along with Robert Hilton and Charles
Pidgeon.   This will was proved by William Bellingham, 7th December, 1693;
power being reserved to the other executors.   But before the will was proved
William Bellingham brought a bill of complaint in the Court of Chancery, as
executor of his brother Alan.   After rehearsing the provisions of the will,
which made him joint executor along with Hilton and Pidgeon, and mentioning
the debt of £13,000, he goes on to say: "After making the said will and deeds

of trust the said Allan, with his said trustees, Pidgeon and Hilton, for the consideration of £24,400 sold the manor of Levens and all other his lands, etc., in Westmorland, to James Graham, Esq., and his heirs, who had a mortgage of the premises for about £13,000, in the name of Richard Graham, Esq., which by agreement he was to retain out of the purchase money. And the rest of the purchase money (which included £200 for goods in the manor house of Levens) was paid to the said Trustees towards payment of the rest of the debts of the said Allan. But all timber trees of full growth in Barrow-field, etc., parcel of the premises, were excepted out of the purchase." So far as this can be made clear, it seems that William Bellingham was objecting to the sale. The result, however, was that Levens irrevocably passed away. Nearly 100 years later a grandson of Mrs. Johnson, Alan Johnson, of Wakefield, in Yorkshire, entered into correspondence with William Bellingham (afterwards Sir William Bellingham, Bart.), who had just gone into Parliament. He sent him some interesting letters which had passed between his grandfather, Alexander Johnson, of Preston, and Col. Bellingham, the diarist, and his son Henry, in the years 1701, 1720, 1725, and 1726, showing that the cousinship was acknowledged many years after the Colonel's stay in Lancashire. In speaking of Levens passing away he says: "Alan, who followed the fortunes of King James the 2nd, spent his estate, and died at St. Germains, in France, in 1692. [This must be an error for 1693.] He must have been a weak man to hazard his life and fortune in such a cause, which made it suspected he was gulled out of his estate; but his next brother (though of the Law) hated his memory so much that he would make no enquiry. This is the tradition." Here we see tradition was wrong, for William Bellingham certainly did make enquiry, though it seems to have been ineffectual. Later on, in 1696, he brought a bill of complaint against Sir Thomas Rawlinson, Knt. So far as can be made out, it refers to certain deeds executed some years before; but the most interesting item is the evidence of one Anthony Saul, of Pincaster, who deposed that he had been present at a trial at Appleby Assizes, some three years ago, between James Grahame, Esq., and one George Jopson, and that he had heard one Matthew King give evidence upon oath "that Allan Bellingham, the plaintiff's late brother, was dead, and that he dyed in France, and that he heard the said Matthew King say that he had been upon the said Allan Bellingham's grave in France." This is all that is known about the ultimate fate of one whom Machell calls "an ingenious but unhappy young man." His portrait, by Sir Peter Lely, passed to his sister, Mary Johnson, and was in the possession of her grandson Alan, along with one of herself by the same artist, in 1787. From him these came to J. W. D. Johnson, Esq., of Sarre Court, in Kent, who sold them to Sir Henry Bellingham.

William Bellingham was of Lincoln's Inn, and practised as a barrister. He married Elizabeth, daughter of Dutton, third Lord Gerard, by his second wife, Lady Elizabeth O'Bryen, daughter and co-heir of Henry, fifth Earl of Thomond, and widow of William Spencer, of Ashton, in Lancashire, third son of William Lord Spencer. By her first husband, Mr. Spencer, she had a daughter, Elizabeth, who married Robert Hesketh, of Rufford, in Lancashire; by her second, Mr. Bellingham, she had two daughters, Elizabeth, wife of Sir Robert Echlin, Bart., of Rush, in Ireland, who had a daughter and heiress, Elizabeth, who married Francis Palmer, but the issue is extinct; and Dorothy, wife of Sir Roger Bradshaigh, Bart., of Haigh, in Lancashire, who died without issue. Thus eventually the sisters of Alan Bellingham became his co-heiresses.

It is interesting to find the cousinship between Col. Thomas Bellingham and the Levens branch kept up in later years. In a letter dated 27th of February, 1703-4, addressed to Alexander Johnson, he tells him he has spoken on his behalf to the Duke of Ormond, " who, upon my first mentioning of you to be a relation of Mr. Keightley's, and your Lady a relation of mine, he readily promised to use his interest with the Queen, that you should be made high Sherriffe of Yorkshire for the ensuing year, and commanded me to leave a memorandum of it with Mr. Secretary Southwell." He subscribes himself " Your affectionate kinsman and most faithful servant, THO. BELLINGHAM." In a postscript he adds, " I could wish you could send me a good clean dayry mayd, for I want one very much, and I would give any reasonable wages." Addressed to " ALEXANDER JOHNSON, Esq., att Preston, Lancashire." The Colonel's son, Henry Bellingham, writes to Mr. Johnson, 27th of August, 1701, addressing him as " Dear Cos," and goes on to say he is harassed with business, " for to-morrow I am to run a little Grey Mare of mine against a Gelding of my Lord Mount Alexander's (one of the Lords Justices) for a hundred guineas," and observes, " My mare has run 5 races and never was beaten." He ends, " Your's (in Jockey haste) Intirely, HEN. BELLINGHAM." In 1720 he writes again, and reference is made to the evident failure in the health of the old Colonel, who died in 1721. After speaking of the death of his wife's mother, Mrs. Moore, he says, " to aggravate my concern my Father has been very much out of order this week past, but I hope in God he will gett over it. He took your letter very kindly; and, as we have a great regard for you all, he joins with me in most hearty kind remembrances to all our Relations and Friends on your side the water. I am sorry to find my Cousin William Bellingham forgott he had any such here. My Father and I design to send you 4 Bottles of the right Drogheda usquebagh whenever Mr. Ward (?) has an opportunity of conveying it to you, to whom I enclose this, and if you could gett me 2 or 3 couple of Whelps (for I would choose them rather than old Doggs, because few people care to part with good ones out of their Parks) of the finest best Tongued Breed in your Country, you would extreamly oblige, Dear Cousen, your most Affect. Kinsman and Faithfull Humble Servant, HEN. BELLINGHAM. My sister gives her Duty to you, and she hears your Book is in Drogheda and gratefully accepts of it." He had three sisters—Jane (called Jenny in the diary), who married Francis Quin, of Dublin; Abigail, who was born at Preston, during the Colonel's residence there, in 1688; and Anne. Another letter, written 25th of March, 1725, is interesting, because it gives a clue to the death of William Bellingham, about which there is some uncertainty. He says, "As the Family of the Bellinghams are now contracted into a very narrow compass, and there is none to support the name that I know of but 2 sons that I have, it endears me the more to all of that Family that are surviving. I hear my Cozen Will has left 2 Daughters, and, if my Coz. his Widdow is as fond of propogating the name as I am, sure no consideration of fortune should withhold me from it. I thank God I have a competent one, and one of the sweetest seats, perhaps, in this Kingdome, so if you think proper to communicate this to Coz. Dolly Bellingham, Coz. Patten, etc. (to all whom my most hearty love and service), and let me know their sentiments upon it, it may chance to be satisfactory and fortunate to us all, which is all that is aimed at by, Dear Coz., your most affect. Kinsman and Humble Servant, HEN. BELLINGHAM." One more letter, dated 15th of November, 1726, closes the series. After thanking Mr. Johnson for some "Puppys" he had sent, but which were "so poor and mangey with their long voyage that I fear I shall scarce recover them," he says, "It is a great concern to me that my affairs are so circumstanced, having a publick Employment, besides the care of my Estate and Family, that I almost despair of seeing my Friends in England, but particularly sweet Preston, where I spent so many days (?) of innocent . . . but I believe few or none of my Relations or Acquaintance except yourself are alive. . . . This is a day of humiliation, abstinence, and thanksgiving for the great Deliverance I had this day twelvemonth for the next to a miraculous preservation of my life, at the same time it was fatal to my unhappy Antagonist. I lament still as a misfortune, but which I hope won't be imputed to me as a Crime. I pray God preserve all my Friends from such a Disaster, but if it should befall them may they have . . . to plead in their

Justification. I wish your Neeces could see Castle Bellingham as I have improved it. I fancy they would scarcely meet with many sweeter places in England, as most who have seen it declare, and how glad should I be to see you and any Friends here; but that is a happiness I am afraid I must despair. If I had any expectation of success, I would send my Son over, who is a gentle, clever Person of a Man, and has many very good qualifications, besides the superficial one of Dancing, etc." He alludes to a duel he had to fight with a Mr. Tisdall, at Dunleer. It arose from an election squabble. Tisdall, who was a noted swordsman, fastened a quarrel on Mr. Bellingham, who was compelled to draw his sword in self-defence, and was fortunate enough to kill instead of being killed. At the inquest he was acquitted at once by the evidence of those who witnessed the affair. The son, also called Henry, did not marry one of Mr. Johnson's nieces, but chose Miss Margaret Henry, the daughter of a rich Dublin banker. He had no children by her, and died in 1755, when his brother Alan succeeded and had a large family.

Mr. Bellingham's partiality for his country place was well justified. Mrs. Delany, wife of the Dean of Down, in a letter dated 24th of August, 1745, to her sister, Mrs. Dewes, describing her journey from Co. Down to Delville, near Dublin, says, "Dined at a place called Castle Bellingham, one of the prettiest places I have seen in Ireland." The original Castle, which had belonged to the Gernons was destroyed by King James' troops, as is related in the diary. The ruins remaining are only a few fragments, and no doubt were used as a quarry, when the Colonel built the present house about fifty yards distant. But no one who saw what he built between 1690 and 1700 would recognise it in the Castle of the present day. The late Sir Alan Bellingham, who had heard a description of it from those who personally remembered it, said it was a sort of Dutch chateau, with a high pitched roof, strongly resembling Beaulieu, in Co. Louth, which was built about the same time. The execrable taste of the latter part of the 18th century lowered the roof, and made it a commonplace three-storied house. " Strawberry Hill Gothic " castellated it in the early part of the 19th century, and later additions have made it much more commodious and dignified, but such as the Colonel would certainly not recognise as his construction. The grounds were also laid out in the Dutch taste, with formal avenues of limes, of which one remains nearly perfect, and canals of which tokens are left, all in keeping with the architecture of the house. The demesne was planted extensively with oaks and beeches which, with the beautiful river Glyde, served to make it well worth the praises of its owner and Mrs. Delany. Tradition says that the

Colonel, during the building of his house, occupied one, which is now a shop, in the adjoining village. It is worthy of note that the place hitherto called Gernonstown received the name of Castle Bellingham towards the close of the 17th century. The Colonel's father, the grantee of the estate, describes himself in his will, dated 8th of December, 1676, as "Henry Bellingham, of Gernonstown, Esq." He left £50 to his sister, "Lady Jane Gilbert, wife unto Sir George Gilbert, Knt.;" £100 to his daughter, Anne Bickerton, widow; and made his son Thomas sole executor. It was proved on the 5th of April, 1677.

The Colonel styles himself in his will, dated 30th of April, 1716, "Thomas Bellingham of Castle Bellingham Esq." He desires to be buried "privately, without pomp, scarf, or scutcheon, in the vault of the chappell of Castle Bellingham." He speaks of being seized in fee in his own right and possessed of and in the lands called Clinton lands, in the town lands of Adamstown and Williamstown in Co. Louth, and the town land of Bolies, and of a considerable personal estate. He leaves to his daughter, Anne Bellingham, on her marriage, £500, and meanwhile £30 per annum; to his daughter, Abigail Bellingham, £500. He makes his son, Henry Bellingham, and his beloved kinsman, Robert Sibthorpe, of Dunany, his executors. By a codicil he left the interest of leased lands in Drumboal and Annis, Co. Monaghan, between his daughters. He does not mention his daughter Jane, who no doubt was provided for on her marriage with Francis Quin, in 1692. The will was proved on the 5th of June, 1722.

Family papers, wills, and the diary, are almost the sole means of bringing us into personal contact with the Colonel. His portrait, by Jervas, was evidently taken when he was well advanced in life, and represents him as a somewhat coarse-featured, good-humoured looking man, disguised in the huge flowing wig of the period, and presenting a striking contrast to the much more handsome and refined face of his spendthrift cousin Alan. His wife, Abigail, was no beauty, and looking at her picture one cannot be surprised at two out of the three daughters remaining single. Unfortunately the portrait of the son, Henry, who was born at Twyford, in Co. Westmeath, 1675, was lost early in the last century. His wife, Mary Moore, whom he married in 1700, was the first to bring good looks into the family, and she added nearly 20 quarterings to its escutcheon, her father, Thomas Moore, of the Drogheda family, representing, through the Brents of Charing, in Kent, a branch of the Berkeleys, of Beverstone. Her two sisters, Anne and Elizabeth, co-heirs with herself, married respectively Henry Tenison, of Dillonstown, Co. Louth, and, as second wife, Dacre Barrett Lernard, of Belhus, in Essex.

The Colonel's two unmarried daughters, Anne and Abigail, lived far into the 18th century. Anne's will was proved 26th of March, 1759. It must have been made quite 20 years previous, because she mentions her brother, Henry Bellingham, whose will was proved 22nd of March, 1739-40. She leaves to her " dear sister Bellingham," i.e., her sister-in-law, Henry's wife, a " ring with Queen Mary's hair." She makes her " well-beloved sister, Abigail Bellingham," sole executrix. The will was sworn to by her nephew, Thomas Quin, son of her sister Jane. She died on the 21st of April, 1758, and was buried in Castle Bellingham Churchyard, beside her sister-in-law, Mrs. Bellingham, who died on the 10th of July, 1758. Abigail Bellingham's will is dated 6th of May, 1762. She desires to be buried " as I buried my ever dearest sister." She leaves a quantity of small articles of jewellery to various nieces and great-nieces ; to her great-nephew, Henry Bellingham (her nephew Alan's son) she leaves " my grandfather Handcock's picture ;" and " to my great-nephew, Thomas Bickerton, my brother's picture " (i.e., Henry Bellingham, who died in 1740). She added two codicils in 1765, and the will was proved by her nephew, Alan Bellingham, on the 22nd of March, 1770. She was the last survivor of the old Colonel's children, and as she lived till 1770 she must have been personally well known to Miss Alice Bellingham, born in 1749, who lived at Castle Bellingham till 1835, and whose sister Lucy survived till 1839. What they must have heard her say about her father the Colonel, and the Battle of the Boyne, has unfortunately died with them. The late Sir Alan Bellingham, born in 1800, preserved a few fragments of family history which he had gleaned from old people ; but the most surprising fact is that in 1796, when Sir William Bellingham was created a Baronet and wished to record his pedigree, no one seems to have known what was the precise connection between Capt. Henry Bellingham, the Colonel's father, and the Levens branch. Francis Townshend was the Herald employed to trace it, and he perpetrated the most astounding blunder. Having, probably, seen the Colonel's diary, and finding him " calling cousins " with William Bellingham and his sisters, he jumped at the conclusion that his father Henry was identical with Henry Bellingham, younger son of Alan Bellingham, of Levens, by his wife, Susan Constable. This would have made the Colonel first cousin to William and the others. The slightest pains in looking into documents would have shown him that this was an impossibility, as this Henry had an only child Frances, who married Sir Reginald Graham, Bart. But the result was a magnificent parchment pedigree, splendidly emblazoned, giving an utterly erroneous descent, and misleading all the Baronetages down to the present day. It has, however, been set right in Mr. Cokayne's "Complete Baronetage." As if this were not enough, the Heralds' College solemnly confirmed to Sir William and his successors in the Baronetcy the coat-of-arms borne by the Levens branch, without any regard to the fact that a fresh coat had been granted in the 17th century, which appears on the funeral achievement of Robert Bellingham's widow, Margaret, who was buried in 1668 at St. Werburgh's Church, and was the mother of Sir Daniel and Capt. Henry Bellingham. In this case the colours were simply reversed and a fleur de lys added as a mark of cadency. Instead of " argent 3 bugle horns sable, stringed gules, garnished or," the coat was " sable 3 bugle horns argent stringed or," a fleur de lys being placed between the bugle horns. Instead of " a Buck's head couped or," the new crest was " a Buck's head erased sable charged with a fleur de lys or, attired of the last." This was granted 20th of December, 1662. How all this came to be utterly ignored it is impossible to say. One would have thought that Sir William's father, Alan Bellingham, who was born in 1709, and was 12 when his grandfather the Colonel died, would have been able to enlighten his children as to the facts. The four statues which now adorn the terrace at Bellingham Castle, Castle Bellingham, came from Dubber Castle, the seat of Sir Richard Bellingham, who was son of Sir Daniel, and first cousin of the Colonel, and ought to have reminded the family of the connection. Sir Daniel's daughters (Mrs. Frowde, Mrs. Corker, Mrs. Swan, Mrs. Nelmes, Mrs. Boyle, and Lady Pakenham, all first cousins of the Colonel) had families which must have been perfectly well known to the Colonel's son and daughters. Finally, it was reserved for a pedigree of the Swan family, apparently compiled early in the 18th century, which came into the late Sir Alan Bellingham's possession by purchase, to disclose the real facts of the case, and to bring lasting discredit on Mr. Townshend the Windsor Herald's genealogical reputation.

A. R. M.

SITE OF THE ORIGINAL BELLINGHAM FAMILY SEAT,

at Bellingham, in Northumberland; now only a mound.

PREFATORY NOTE.

The castle or original residential stronghold of the Bellingham family was at Bellingham, in Northumberland. Long ago—probably much anterior to the Derwentwater possession—in consequence of military attacks, or through being abandoned as a family seat, the castle fell into ruins. According to local tradition, it stood in what is now a field, on the Haggerston estate, between the bridge which goes over the burn in the centre of Bellingham and the railway station. In the early part of last century a few remains of the ancient structure were visible, but they have since disappeared, and now the site can only be identified by a mound designated by old residents as the Hoe or Castle Hill.

Bellingham Chapel, in Kendal Parish Church, was built in the time of Henry VIII. It occupies two bays, on the east side, of the "Bellingham aisle." There used to be in one corner of this chapel a box tomb, bearing memorial brasses. Many years ago the stones forming the tomb were removed, and the brasses were—so it has been alleged—"purloined." The brasses related to Sir Roger Bellingham of Burneside, Margaret his wife, and their granddaughter Thomasine, wife of Sir William Thornburgh; two effigies (figures of a man and a woman) were also represented in brass; and at each corner of the stone an escutcheon appeared in similar metal. The brass pertaining to Sir Roger and his wife bore the following inscription:—" Here under lyeth Sir Roger Bellingham, Knt. (which of his own proper costs and charges builded the Chapell of our Lady within this church of Kendall), and Margaret his wife, daur of Sir Robt. Aske, Knight, and of Elizabeth his wife, daur to the Lord John Clifford, now created Earl of Cumberland, which Sir Roger died the 18th day of July, A.D., 1533, and the sd Margaret dyed the day of   , A.D., 15   , whose souls Jhesu pardon." (Whitaker's " History of Richmondshire.") On a freestone panel, inserted in a pillow at the head of the tomb, north side, there were representations of arms, quartered, relating to the Bellingham family and Burneshead. (Nicholson's "Annals of Kendal.") In a pew, conjectured to have been that of the Bellingham family, there was an effigy, in brass, of Sir Alan Bellingham, in armour. When the church was restored (1850-52) this brass was put in the north wall of the ancient Bellingham quire. It contains the following inscription:—"Here lyeth the bodye of Alan Bellingham, Esquier, who maryed Catheryan, daughter of Anthonye Ducket, Esquier, by whom he had no children, after whose decease he maryed Dorothie, daughter of Thomas Sanford, Esquier, of whom he had vij sonnes and eight daughters, of which 5 sonnes and 7 daughters with ye said Dorothie ar yeat lyving. He was thre score and one yarre of age, and dyed ye 7 of Maye, A.M. 1577 (A.B.D.)." Against the walls of the Bellingham chapel there are suspended an old helmet and a sword, said to have belonged to Sir Roger Bellingham; but there is a tradition which ascribes the ownership of the helmet to a Royalist officer— Major Philipson (whose soubriquet was "Robin the Devil"), of Belle Isle, Windermere. At the time the church was restored the Bellingham chapel was completely re-roofed, and the old, elaborate oak ceiling, then very considerably decayed, was supplanted by a new one of similar design, in imitation of the rich fretwork, and stalactic ornamentation of the same period, in stone. It was also adorned with gilt bosses, containing bugle horns and other bearings, the cognizances of the Bellingham family. At the same time the organ was placed in the Bellingham chapel (Nicholson's "Annals"). In 1863 the Bellingham tomb was restored, and the brasses "were renewed by the late John Broadbent, Esq., of London, a descendant of the family." (Robson's "Guide to Kendal," &c.). The chapel is now the sole property of the Kendal Parish Church authorities, and is kept in repair by them. In 1692 Burneside Hall, when visited by the Rev. Thomas Machell, was evidently a substantial and imposing place. The structure consisted of "a court with a lodge and battlements, through which was the ascent into the hall," whilst "before the court was a large pond on each side of the passage to the gate; and on either side a small island, with a tree planted in the midst." For a long time the hall has been in a ruinated state. Upwards of 70 years ago it was described as "a fine old ruin," "occupied by a farmer." (Fisher's "Picturesque Illustrations of Westmorland.") Part of the great tower and a gateway still remain entire. Portions of the old building "have been utilised in the present farm-house, and much has no doubt entirely disappeared." (Robson's "Guide to Kendal," &c.)

BELLINGHAM CHAPEL

(corner to right)
in Kendal Parish Church.

BELLINGHAM CHOIR

(corner to right)
in Bellingham Church.

The Bellingham and Strickland families had respectively a town house at Kendal; that of the former being at the top of Stramongate, and that of the latter at the bottom of the same street. The house which the Bellinghams had here is now used as a shop. In it are various ancient and curious articles, including two carved oak chimney pieces, a cupboard of carved oak (on which are represented the triple hunting horns of the Bellingham family), several documents, &c. Levens Hall is now and has for several years been in the possession of Captain Josceline Bagot.

Thomas Bellingham, the diarist, was connected with the forces of William III. He was quartered with his regiment for some time in Lancashire—chiefly at Preston. In August, 1689, he left Preston with his regiment, and, joining the forces named, at Hoylake, sailed with them to Ireland. In November, 1689, he returned to Preston, and remained there till May, 1690, when he again left—embarking with soldiers, &c., at Hoylake—for Ireland. He acted as a guide or A.D.C. when William's army marched from Dundalk to the Boyne, was consulted by both William and the Duke of Schomberg before the battle of the Boyne took place, was at that battle, ranked as Colonel then or shortly afterwards, and went with the King to Duleek. Later he withdrew from military life. On the 15th of September, 1721, he died, at the age of 75, and his remains were interred under the Protestant Episcopal Church at the village of Castlebellingham, in a vault which it is said he had "caused to be made for himself and his parents." The present owner of Castlebellingham is Sir Henry Bellingham, fourth baronet, who succeeded his father, Sir Alan Edward Bellingham, on the death of the latter in 1889. Sir Henry was born in 1846. He is a M.A., Oxon, qualified as a barrister-at-law, is private chamberlain to His Holiness Pope Pius X., and held a similar post under the two previous Pontiffs, is a Commissioner of National Education, Ireland, a senator of the Royal University, and was M.P. for Co. Louth from 1880 to 1885. He has been twice married—first, in 1874, to Constance, daughter of the second Earl of Gainsborough, who died in 1891, the issue being two sons and two daughters; and secondly, in 1895, to the Hon. Lelgarde Clifton, younger daughter of Augustus Wykeham Clifton, Esq., of Warton Hall, near Lytham, and the 23rd Baroness Grey de Ruthyn. The issue of the first marriage was— eldest son, Edward, Lt. Royal Scots; second son, Roger, Lt. R.A.; eldest daughter, Ida, a nun of the order of the Holy Child; second, Augusta, married John, fourth Marquis of Bute. The marriage of this latter was solemnised in the parish church of Kilsaran, near Castlebellingham, on the 6th of July, 1905. After the ceremony, which was a very picturesque one, the bride and bridegroom (accompanied by the wedding guests and a number of pipers and drummers) drove to Annagassan landing stage, from which there was a procession of boats, headed by a barge containing the newly-married couple, to a steam yacht in the bay. The Marquis of Bute had specially chartered this yacht, and by it he took his bride to Scotland. Amongst the varied and valuable heirlooms in the castle are numerous family portraits, ranging down from the time of Queen Elizabeth ; some Stuart relics ; a wine or liqueur case, presented by William III. to Colonel Thomas Bellingham ; a knife, fork, and spoon used by his Majesty on the day before the battle of the Boyne ; and the diary of the Colonel.

The period covered by the diary is a little over two years, namely, from August 1st, 1688, to September 12th, 1690. Whilst with his regiment, at Preston, Colonel Bellingham brought his wife and family to that town, in which he had some cousins of the Bellingham stock. He appears to have had a very lively, sociable time in Preston and neighbourhood, adhering closely to the modes and habits of life which were then fashionable. He moved amongst the higher and more influential sections of the community, including members of county families. The diary is, in size, something like an old-fashioned, stiff-backed, clasp pocket-book : it is about $6\frac{1}{2}$in. deep, $4\frac{1}{4}$in. broad, and three-quarters of an inch thick (outside measurement). Bound richly and strongly, it is kept in a satchel of ruby velvet, gold embroidered, and, considering its age, it is in really excellent condition. All the entries are in the Colonel's own handwriting, very small and neat ; the phraseology is concise and direct ; and the spelling, though not infrequently of the phonetic order, is far less pronounced or defective in this respect than that met with in many contemporary manuscripts, &c. Lord Macaulay, in his " History of England," mentions " the Bellingham MS." (i.e., the diary of Colonel Bellingham) as being amongst his " chief materials " for the history of the battle of the Boyne. Extracts from the diary have at different periods been printed ; but now, for the first time, it is published in complete form (with explanatory notes).

The punctuation in the diary is irregular, and in many parts it is absent entirely : that adopted in the transcript is based on modern principles. Where mile distances are given in notes relating to places, &c., in Ireland, they are of English length. The copyright of the diary belongs to Sir Henry Bellingham.

A journal, kept by one of the members of the Fleetwood family—presumably Edward—of Penwortham Hall, near Preston, and covering about three years in the latter part of the 17th century, makes frequent reference to the diarist. By this journal it appears that Fleetwood and Bellingham were on very friendly terms, and that the latter was staying at Preston in 1687, or upwards of 12 months before the commencement of his diary. In the first portion of the journal Bellingham is styled "Mr.," then "Mr. Tho.," and subsequently, to the end of it, "Capt.," Bellingham—the Colonelcy having evidently been conferred some time after 1689. An entry in the journal, for December 15th, 1689, states that Fleetwood stood godfather on that day for "Capt. Bellingham's daughter Eliz.," and that she was "christened ith' house"—a circumstance, no doubt, due to the fact that the father was, according to his diary, kept indoors through a fever of some kind from which he had been suffering. Owing to the same cause, there is a break in the diary from November 22nd to the 13th of the following January, with an intermediately written note saying that "Betty [Elizabeth] was borne ye 12 of Dec., between 8 and 9 at night." As far as it goes, Fleetwood's journal, which has not been published, strikingly confirms the accuracy of the Bellingham diary.

My thanks are especially due to Sir Henry Bellingham for facilities given to me in transcribing the Bellingham diary, as well as supplying various photographs, &c.; to the Rev. Canon Maddison, of Lincoln, for contributing the introduction, tabular pedigrees, and sundry note items; to Captain Bagot, of Levens Hall, for views exterior and interior, of that interesting mansion; and to Mr. H. W. Clemesha, of Preston, for valuable revisional assistance.

A. H.

June, 1908.

The Bellingham Diary.

August ye 1st, 1688. Preston.

A fayr day. The Duke of Somersett came to this town, upon whom the Mayor and Corporation waited in their formallityes, and gave him a noble banquett and wine, and made him and Mr. Cholmondeley, of Vale Royall, and 2 other Gentlemen, free of the Corporation. I was invited with Coll. Rawstorn to supp with him, where we had some discourses about a Parliament, etc.

Alderman Nicholas Walmsley was the Mayor of Preston at this time.—There is no mention made in the Corporation records of either the banquet or the freedom-granting.—The Duke of Somerset would be Charles sixth Duke, who married Lady Elizabeth the celebrated heiress of the "ancient and historical Percies." He held very important positions in the Courts of Charles II., William III., and Queen Anne, and died in 1748, at the age of 87.—Mr. Cholmondeley would probably be Hugh Cholmondeley, who favoured and forwarded the Revolution, and was, on the accession of William and Mary, created an earl. If not Hugh, then in all likelihood the gentleman alluded to would be George Cholmondeley, a commanding officer in the army of William III. at the battle of the Boyne, in 1690.—Coll. Rawstorn was Colonel Laurence Rawstorne, of New Hall, in the parish of Bury, and High Sheriff of Lancashire in 1681. He owned the manor of Hutton, including Hutton Hall, in the parish of Penwortham, near Preston, and was probably on a visit to the Hall at this time. At a subsequent period Hutton Hall became the seat of the Rawstornes. Laurence Rawstorne, High Sheriff of Lancashire in 1814, and Lieutenant-Colonel of the 1st Lancashire Militia, resided for a time at Hutton Hall. After the rebuilding of Penwortham Hall (now called the Priory), in 1832, he removed to that place, and he died there in 1850. Later, it was for several years occupied by his son Laurence, now of Hutton Hall.

Ye 2d.—A fayr day. Chancery Court. R. Rochfort and Mr Ludlow came here. We din'd att Turlagh's. After dinner we went to ye marsh and bowld. Att night were att Rigby's with severall of ye gentlemen of ye town.

> The Palatine Chancery Court at this time sat at Preston.—R. Rochfort was the diarist's brother-in-law, and was for some time Speaker of the Irish House of Commons, subsequently becoming Lord Chief Baron. —Turlagh's was either an inn or a sort of dining and refreshment place.— Ye marsh was Preston Marsh, on the west side of the town.—Att Rigby's: There were two innkeepers of this name in Preston at the time.

Ye 3d.—A fayr day. We went to Lancaster and call'd att Garstin. Saw Lancaster Castle and Church.

> Garstin is intended for Garstang.—Lancaster Castle and the Parish Church near it were probably visited; if not, then they would be noticed from the road on the south side of the town. They would be very conspicuous, picturesque objects as seen from the Greaves, down which the road whereon the diarist would travel takes its course; but now, owing to the structural development of the town and the growth of trees, intermediately, this view is greatly obscured.

Ye 4th.—A fayr day. We went over Carthmell sandes to Levens, and found ye sands boggy and hazardouse. We reached Levens before dinner. After went to ride a buck, but he broake out of ye parke. From thence we came to ye force, but got no fish. We shott a fatt Buck.

> Over Carthmell sands: This must be a mistake. If the party went from Lancaster to Levens, by way of "Carthmell [Cartmel] sands," they would go many miles out of their proper course. Cartmel sands are between Flookburgh and Bardsea—far distant and virtually at a right angle from the ordinary and the best road between Lancaster and Levens. They may have crossed Lancaster sands and then proceeded along the west side of the Kent estuary, which would be considerably shorter, but still an unnecessarily long, route; or, which is most likely, though needlessly circuitous, the way taken would be across the sands near Milnthorpe, then round the head of the Kent estuary, and so to Levens Hall.—The words "to ride a buck" mean to hunt with hounds, in contrast to the shooting.— The "force" was Levens Force, a cascade or small waterfall—probably one of the two falls mentioned by Camden the antiquary. Thomas Fuller in one of his works also refers to them: from "master Camden" he says he learns that here in the river there are two waterfalls, "whereof the northern, sounding clear and loud, foretokeneth fair weather; the southern, on the same terms, presageth rain"; and he wishes "that the former of these may be vocall in haytime and harvest; the latter, after great drought, that so both of them may make welcome musick for the inhabitants."

Ye 5th.—A hott day.   We went to Hearsham Church, and heard Mr. Ridley preach.   He and ye Schoolmaster Green came to dinner with us.   In the evening we all walk'd into the parke, which is very pleasant and delightfull.   Mr. Tim Bankes came to us, etc.

> Hearsham is intended for Heversham, in which parish Levens is situated. In 1661 Heversham Church was burnt down and the monuments in it destroyed.   Afterwards the church was rebuilt, and inscribed memorial stones were placed in it by the Bellinghams of Levens and others.—Mr. Ridley was the Vicar of Heversham.—Green would be the master of Heversham School, a noted educational establishment, founded in 1613 by Edward Wilson, Esq., of Nether Levens, ancestor of the Wilsons of Dallam Tower, near Milnthorpe.—As to Mr. Tim Banks, he was probably a local person, or from Kendal.

Ye 6th.—A hott day.   We rode to Hersam Head and view'd ye fine Country about.   Went to the force.   Saw fish taken severall wayes.   After dinner bowl'd with severall of the neighbours. Sweetman, a youth of a good fortune, din'd with us.

> Hersam Head, i.e., Heversham Head, is north-east of and a short distance · from the Church.   Fine views can be obtained from its summit of Farleton Knot, Morecambe Bay, the Lake mountains, &c.

Ye 7th.—Some raine this morning.   We rode and saw ye colts. After dinner we went to Kendall, where we were handsomely entertain'd by Mrs. North and her sonne and by Mr. Joseph Sympson.

Ye 8th.—Much raine this morning.   We hunted an outlyer and brought him into ye parke and kill'd him, after seeing admirable sport both by land and water.   We bowl'd all the afternoon with Dr. Tarleton, etc.

> An outlyer would be a deer separated from the herd—one detached from the park and alone.

Ye 9th.—A fayr day.   We din'd att Crookelands.   Saw Sawney Farrington.   Dranke a bowl of Punch and came home in good time.

> Crookelands is a small, hamlet-like place about two and a half miles east

of Heversham.—Sawney (a nick-name corrupted from Sandy, i.e., Alexander) Farrington would presumably be related to the Faringtons of Worden Hall, in the parish of Leyland.

Ye 10th.—A fayr but windy day. We left Levens about 8 in ye morning, Din'd att Lancaster, Call'd at Garstin [Garstang], and reach'd Preston between 8 and 9.

Ye 11th.—Some showers. I was with Sr. Tho. Clifton, Mr. Fleetwood, and others, and in ye evening bowld.

Sir Thomas Clifton was of Westby and Clifton. He was created a baronet in 1660. In 1694 he was charged with high treason, but acquitted. He died about two months afterwards, when the baronetcy became extinct.—Mr. Fleetwood was Mr. Edward Fleetwood, of Penwortham, son of John Fleetwood, of Penwortham, who died in 1657—a descendant of John Fletewoode (son and heir of William Fletewoode, of Heskin), who was the lessee of Penwortham Priory from the Abbot and Convent of Evesham, and subsequently purchased the reversion thereof from the Crown; the grant being confirmed in 6 Elizabeth, 1563.

Ye 12th.—A fayr day. Ye Curate preached twice. In ye afternoone we walkd to Avenham garden.

Mr. Farrand was the Curate of Preston—one of the stipendiary or "parish chaplain" kind—at this time. His name occurs in the proceedings of the Preston Common Council under the date of July 19th, 1687, at which time or shortly afterwards he was appointed Stipendiary Curate of the Parish Church; the Council sanctioning an allowance to him, from the town's revenue, of £20 per year.—Avenham Garden (not in existence now) was on the north side of Avenham-lane, between the present Bairstow-street and Avenham-road.

Ye 13th.—A fayr day. Mr. Fleetwood, Coll. Rawstorn, Mr. Hodgkinson, &c. Din'd on a venison Pasty. I bowld in ye afternoon. Ye fayr was proclaim'd.

Mr. Fleetwood and Colonel Rawstorn have already been sufficiently identified.—Mr. Hodgkinson was Alderman Thomas Hodgkinson, who was Mayor of Preston in 1673 and 1680, and died in 1697. He belonged to a family which had been most conspicuously associated with the public life of Preston, and, in a municipal or corporately representative sense, he was the last of his line.—The fayr was a very old-established yearly fair. It is first definitely mentioned in a Charter granted to Preston by King John in 1199. By that Charter it is called "a Free Fair." It lasted eight days, and till the reign of Edward III. was the only fair held in the borough.

BURNESIDE HALL,

Near Kendal,

Where the first Bellingham who went permanently south married and settled.

Ye 14th.—A fayr day.   I saw Mr. Rushton's bond and articles sign'd and seal'd and sent to London.   Ye beast fair.   I bowl'd in ye afternoon.   Mr. Fleetwood, Houghton, Blundell, &c.

> Rushton is here a variant of Rishton, and the gentleman whose bond and articles are referred to was, no doubt, Alderman Ralph Rishton, who had for a considerable time been connected with the Preston postal service.—The beast fair was the horse and cattle fair, held in the early part of the time previously mentioned.   Houghton would be Benjamin, brother of Sir Charles Hoghton, fourth baronet, who was in 1688-89 M.P. or Knight of the Shire for the County of Lancaster—a position he had occupied in two previous Parliaments.   He resided at Hoghton Tower, near Preston, and died there in 1710.—Blundell was one of a family of this name long associated with Preston, and directly or collaterally connected with the Blundells of Ince Blundell in the parish of Sefton : he would be John or his brother Henry, or a son of the latter.

Ye 15th.—A hott day.   Ye horse fayr continues.   There are great store of horses and black cattle, but very cheap.   I was with Mr. Fleetwood and others att ye green.

> Ye green was a bowling green, on the Marsh, and presumably in or near the west corner of it.

Ye 16th.—Much raine in ye afternoon.   Mrs. Patten was marryed this day to Sr. Tho. Stanley, and Chas. Rigby walkd with me in Enam Garden, and discoursed about E. B.   Att night I saw a farce call'd Ye Devil and ye Pope.

> Mrs. Patten was Miss Patten.   Miss is contracted from Mistress, called Mis'ess.   Formerly Miss was written Mis ; and in even the first half of the 18th century it was the practice in cultured, refined society to designate an unmarried lady as Mrs.   The " Mrs " Patten mentioned by the diarist was Elizabeth, only daughter and heiress of Thomas Patten, one of the M.P.'s for Preston in 1688-89.   He resided at Patten House, a mansion which was situated on the north side of the lower part of Church-street, Preston.   The issue of the marriage referred to included Edward Stanley, who was born at Patten House, became the fifth baronet, was M.P. for Lancaster in 1727 and 1734-36, and succeeded as eleventh Earl of Derby on February 1st, 1735-36. Patten House was brought into the Stanley family by the marriage ; for many years it was the Preston town residence of members thereof,—indeed, it was virtually set apart for that purpose till about 1835, when it was pulled down.—Charles Rigby was a son of Edward Rigby, serjeant-at-law, &c.—

Eanam garden was Avenham Garden, already located.—The farce was, no doubt, one played in Preston Theatre. The earliest located theatre in the town was at the south end of the present Woodcock's-court, off Fishergate, and it used to be called the Playhouse.

Ye 17th.—Some raine. I treated Nabby and Betty att a play, and was att night with Mr. Winkly, Lemon, Chaddok.

Nabby was the diarist's wife—née Abigail Handcock, of Twyford, Ireland.—Betty was the diarist's married sister, Mrs. Bickerton, her husband being Robert Bickerton, of Cantiluff, county Armagh.—The play would be at the Theatre.—Winkly was Alderman Thomas Winckley, who was Mayor of Preston four times.—Lemon was William Lemon, gentleman, and a relative of Thomas Winckley. He (Lemon) was an Alderman of Preston, and was five times Mayor of the borough. He was never married. In 1724 he died, when nearly 80 years of age.—Chaddok would be Daniel Chaddock, a local gentleman.

Ye 18th.—Some raine in ye morning. In ye afternoon I was 20th. Dr. Roe, Mr. Fleetwood, and Mr. Taylor.

By the words I was 20th the diarist may mean that he was, individually, the 20th in number at a certain social party, or was the 20th in the list of some important bowling match or other game.—Dr. Roe would, it is very likely, be Dr. Richard Wroe, who preached a sermon in Preston Parish Church at the opening of the Guild in 1682, and who afterwards qualified as a burgess of the borough. At that time he held, amongst other positions, one of the curacies at Wigan, under Bishop Pearson, who was the Rector. Some additional particulars concerning Dr. Wroe appear in a note to the diary entry for June 14th, 1689.—Mr. Taylor was, no doubt, the Rev. Z. Taylor referred to in the next note.

Ye 19th.—Some showers this morning. Mr. Birch fell so ill in ye Church after prayers that he was forc't to goe out, and Mr. Taylour of Ormskirk went into the pulpitt and preach'd an excellent sermon. A Scotch man preached in ye afternoon. Nabby and [I] walk'd to ye boathous, and [on returning] sup't att cousen Patten's.

Mr. Birch was the Rev. Thomas Birch, vicar of Preston Parish Church. He was a son of Samuel Birch, gent., of Ardwick, Manchester, and a brother of John Birch, Colonel in the Parliamentary army. Owing to his religious views he did not get on well with the "high" set at the Parish Church, whilst his political opinions roused the hostility of the Tories in the Common Council; but he continued Vicar of Preston till his death, on January 13th, 1699-1700.—Mr. Taylor was the Rev. Zachary Taylor, M.A., son of the Rev. Zachary Taylor, headmaster of Kirkham Grammar School.

He was Vicar of Ormskirk from 1679 to 1693, when he resigned the living. In 1695 he was presented to the rectory of Croston, near Preston, by King William III. In 1703 he died.—The boathous was on the south side of and close to the Ribble—about 250 yards above the present Penwortham bridge. It stood on or quite near to the site of the building which now goes by the name of the Old Boathouse—the building which succeeded the original boathouse mentioned by the diarist, and which was erected in 1696 by either Edward Fleetwood, son of John Fleetwood of Penwortham, or Henry Fleetwood, one of the Parliamentary representatives of Preston in four Parliaments (1708-22); the second named being "the last of the family settled at Penwortham," and it is said that "under the provisions of an Act of Parliament passed in 1748 he sold the Penwortham estates." The correct name of the original boathouse was the Ferry Boat Inn—a name due to the existence, right opposite, of a ferry, the south wharf of which, in a dilapidated state, is still visible. In 1826—the traffic having been diverted by the opening of a new length of highway a little to the west—the license of the inn was transferred to the present Bridge Inn, near the south-west end of Penwortham bridge.—Cousin Patten was Mrs. Patten, née Agnes Bellingham, sister of Alan (who sold Levens) and William Bellingham. She married William Patten, son of Alderman William Patten, Mayor of Preston in 1655-56, and brother of Thomas Patten who was M.P. for Preston in 1688-89.

20th.—A fayr day. I walk'd with Collonell to Penwortham and din'd there. We stayd some time at ye boathous. I saw ye play call'd Duke and no Duke.

The Collonell was Colonel Rawstorne, who would have an easy relationship entrée at Penwortham Hall (where the dining would take place), through having married (third wife) Margery, daughter of Mr. John Fleetwood, who resided there.—The boathous was referred to in the last note.—The play would be at the Theatre previously mentioned.

Ye 21th.—Much raine. We breakfasted att Kellets on venison. In ye afternoon Coll, &c; dranke att ye Talbott.

Kellets would be Alderman John Kellett's, in Church-street. He was twice Mayor of Preston, and died in 1693.—Coll was Colonel Rawstorne.—The Talbott was an inn—presumably either the present Talbot, in Chapel yard, off Friargate, or a house which stood on its site.

Ye 22th.—A fayr day. I din'd and bowl'd att ye march, and att night saw part of play.

Ye 23th.—A very wet afternoon. We heard of Mr. Billington's foot being Gangrea'd by cutting a nayle of a toe. I was with Dr. Lee and some Apothecaryes till it was late, Att Coopers, &c. In ye morning I walk'd to Walton and saw Mr. Houghton, and came home by ye boathous.

Mr. Billington may have been Mr. William Billington, who was, in this and the following year, one of the wardens of Preston Parish Church; and previously as well as subsequently a similar position was occupied by Mr. James Cooper or Cowper, who was probably the gentleman at whose place the diarist and others staid late.—Mr. Houghton would be a brother—in all likelihood Benjamin—of Sir Charles Hoghton, of Hoghton Tower, and the diarist would see him at Walton Hall, near and on the south-west side of the village of Walton-le-Dale. In the latter part of the sixteenth century—about 1592, it has been conjectured—the manor of Walton, including Walton Hall, was surrendered, as a penalty or compensation for bloodshed, by the Langtons to the Hoghtons. For many years the Hall was more or less occupied by members of the Hoghton family. It was pulled down in 1834, and afterwards another building, called Walton Hall, was erected and chiefly occupied for estate purposes a little to the north-west of its site.—The diarist would return by a bridle path, starting opposite the old Hall, going along the west side of the Darwen to the point where it flows into the Ribble, and so forward, on the south bank of the latter, to the Boathouse, where he would cross, by the ferry, to the Preston side. There is a footway now, on the line of the old bridle path, from Walton to the south-west end of Penwortham bridge.

Ye 24th.—A fayr day after a wett morning. I bowl'd with Lawyer Pat, and was att night att G. Ratliffs.

The lawyer referred to was Thomas Patten (son of Alderman Patten), who was a barrister-at-law.—G. Ratcliff, or George Ratcliffe, appears to have been a local innkeeper. It is not at all unlikely that George Ratcliffe, of Alston, near Preston, who died in or about 1727, was related to him; and both were probably descendants or relatives of Ralph Radcliffe, who owned an estate in the township of Dilworth, about a couple of miles north-east of Alston. In a lane near Written Stone farm, in Dilworth, there is a very large oblong stone, bearing this inscription, cut deeply: "Ravffe Radcliffe laide this stone to lye for ever A.D. 1655." Tradition says that a murder was committed in this lane some hundreds of years ago, and that the stone was placed by Ralph Radcliffe on or opposite where it was perpetrated, "to appease the angry spirit of the victim," which, it was alleged, was in the habit of appearing there.

Ye 25th.—A fayr day. I was with Mr. Fleetwood, 2 Mr. Livesyes, and others att Turlaghs, and after att ye Green.

> The Livesyes would be Ralph Livesey, of Livesey Hall, near Blackburn, and Ralph his only surviving son—the issue of a second marriage with Anne, daughter of Thomas Clayton, of Fulwood, near Preston.—The Green means the bowling green—that on the Marsh, before referred to, no doubt.

Ye 26th.—Much raine in ye morning. After dinner one Shirly, a raw young fellow, preacht. We had this day ye B.pp of Rochesters letter to ye Eccl. Comrs. desiring to be excus'd his attendance att ye board.

> The preaching was at Preston Parish Church. Shirley was not clerically connected with the Church here, and seems to have been quite a stranger temporarily engaged or permitted to preach.—The Bishop of Rochester was Thomas Sprat, and his letter would, of course, be either read or shown, for perusal, in the Church. Copies of it were printed and circulated. Under date August 23rd, 1688, John Evelyn thus refers to the letter in his diary:—
> "Dr. Sprat, Bishop of Rochester, wrote a very honest and handsome letter to the Commissioners Ecclesiastical, excusing himselfe from sitting any longer among them, he by no meanes approving of their prosecuting the Cleargy who refus'd to reade the Declaration for liberty of conscience, in prejudice of the Church of England." Sprat joined the new Ecclesiastical Commission of James II. in 1686. Prior to writing the letter referred to he had "pleaded that his name was inserted in the Commission without his knowledge and during his absence at Salisbury." He died in 1713, and was buried in Westminster Abbey.

Ye 27th.—A close, sultry day. We dind att Coll. Rawstornes. After dinner went with Mr. Fleetwood to Bowles. Cousen [Spr]inghams came here this morning.

> To Bowles, of course, means that the diarist and Mr. Fleetwood, of Penwortham, went a-bowling.—Later entries in the diary clearly justify the letters within brackets [Spr]. This was a cousin on the Gilbert side.

Ye 28th.—A fayr but cloudy day. I din'd with cousens att theyr Lodging. I agreed [made arrangements] for them att Mrs. Taylours. In ye afternoon we were att ye bowling green, and att night I treated them att a bowl of Punch.

> The cousins were obviously the Springhams.

Ye 29th.—A fayr day. Most of ye town are gone to Lancaster Assizes. My Cousens and I bowl'd with Mr. Walmsley, cousen Johnson, and others, and walk'd in ye evening.

> At this time, and for long afterwards, very much preliminary legal work in connection with the Assizes was done at Preston; indeed all or the great bulk of such work, for Lancashire, was done here; and the entire Assize Court business of the county was transacted at Lancaster Castle (not until many years later were Assize Courts opened at Liverpool and Manchester); so that when Assize time came round, as it did twice a year, there was a great exodus of lawyers, their clerks, &c., from Preston to Lancaster.—Mr. Walmsley would be the Rev. George Walmsley, Vicar of Leyland, who was presented to the living there, a few years before, by the diarist's friend, Edward Fleetwood, of Penwortham.—Cousin Johnson was Mrs. Johnson (née Mary Bellingham), the wife of Alexander Johnson, of Rishton or Riston Grange, in the East Riding of Yorkshire, and brother of Martha Johnson, who became the wife of Robert Blundell, a Preston gentleman who died in or about 1670.

Ye 30th.—A very wett morning. In ye afternoon we dranke my cousen Patten's farewell, att cousen Johnsons, with ye Springhams.

Ye 31st.—Much raine in ye morning. After dinner ye Springhams came to me and play'd att tables. I layd a bottle of sack with Dr. Lee yt Belgrade was taken before this day.

> The old name for the game modernly called backgammon was tables.— Belgrade is the city of that name. It was captured by the Austrian army on Sept. 6th, 1688.—Dr. Lee was probably Dr. Charles Leigh, historian of Lancashire, &c., on a visit to the town. He was a native of Singleton, about a dozen miles on the north-west side of Preston.—Sack was a Spanish wine of the dry kind—sherry, or something like it.

September ye 1st.

A very fayr day. In ye morning I walkd to Walton Hall, and in ye afternoon I went with Mr. Houghton and ye Springhams to ye boathouse to meete Mr. Fleetwoods.

> The persons and places here mentioned have already been referred to.— Hereafter, as a rule, no allusion will be made in notes to persons and places already identified or described.

Ye 2d.—A fayr day.   Ye vicar preached and administered the H :
Eu :   In ye evening we walkd to Enam.

> The vicar was the Rev. Thomas Birch of the Parish Church.—H: Eu: i.e.,
> Holy Eucharist.—Enam was Avenham.

Ye 3d.—A fayr day, but much raine att night.   L. C. J. Wright
and judge Jenner came here from Lancaster assize.   I was with Mr.
Fleetwood and others att Rigby's, &c.

> L. C. J. Wright was Lord Chief Justice (Sir Robert) Wright. In 1668 he
> was elected M.P. for King's Lynn ; in 1684-5 he was appointed Recorder of
> Cambridge; after Monmouth's rebellion he accompanied Judge Jeffreys on
> the western assizes ; in 1687 he became Lord Chief Justice of the King's
> Bench ; in 1688 he presided at the trial of the seven Bishops ; near the end
> of the same year he was impeached for high treason ; and in 1689 he died of
> fever in Newgate.—Judge Jenner was Sir Thomas Jenner.   After being
> appointed Recorder of the City of London, by Charles II., made King's
> Serjeant, and elected M.P. for Rye, he was in 1686 raised to the Bench as a
> Baron of the Exchequer. In 1687 he was appointed a Royal Commissioner,
> along with Lord Chief Justice Wright and Cartwright Bishop of Chester, to
> make an inquiry into certain matters connected with the management of
> Magdalen College, Oxford.   In 1688 he was made a Justice of the Court of
> Common Pleas.   When James II attempted to get out of the country, and
> take refuge in France, Jenner tried to escape with him, but was caught at
> Faversham, and subsequently committed to the Tower on the charge of
> "subverting the Protestant religion and the laws and liberties of the
> country." After being imprisoned for a time he was released ; later he was
> expelled from the Bench ; and in 1707 he died at Petersham.

Ye 4th.—A fayr day.   We waited on the mayor to the judges.
I din'd att Mr. Hodgkinsons with young Parker of Browsam.
There came in Mr. Chetham and Weddall, both lawyer[s], and
very pleasant, free men.

> Waiting on the Mayor, &c., means accompanying his Worship to the place
> probably the White Bull (now Bull and Royal) Hotel—where the Judges were
> staying, on their way from Lancaster Summer Assizes.   It was the custom
> in old times for the Corporation of Preston to entertain, in the Town Hall,
> the Judges on their return from Lancaster Assizes ; and most likely after
> visiting those referred to the Mayor and the gentlemen with him would
> proceed with them to the Town Hall for this purpose.—Young Parker was
> Edward Parker (at this time 30 years of age), son of Thomas Parker, who
> was then alive, of Browsholme Hall, a large mansion in Bowland, about half
> a dozen miles north-west of Clitheroe.   Colonel J. W. Robinson Parker now
> owns and resides at the Hall.

Ye 5th.—A rainy day. We bowld and din'd att ye marsh, and att night I gave my cousen Patten his welcome home, att Rigby's. Betty was very ill.

Ye 6th.—Some raine. We din'd att my cousen Johnson's on a pasty of venison, and att night were handsomely treated att my cousen Pattens att a bowl of Punch. There was with us Sr. Tho. Stanley, Coll Hodgkinson, Winkly, Lemmon, Chaddock, Kellett, Cobb, and ye [Spr]inghams.

> Cobb—all the other persons here mentioned having been previously referred to—would be either Paul Cobb, gent., of Bernard's Inn, or one of his four sons who, with himself, were enrolled in-burgesses of Preston at the Guild in 1682.

Ye 7th.—A wett day. I received some Ortolans from cousen Frowde, and att night I treated all my cousens Johnsons, Pattens, and Springhams.

> Ortolans—small birds of the bunting species, and much esteemed for the delicate flavour of their flesh.—Frowde was a gentleman who had married a daughter of Sir D. Bellingham, the diarist's uncle.

Ye 8th.—A wett day. This evening cousens Springham treated Mr. Fleetwood and severall of us att ye mitree, &c.

> Ye mitree was the Mitre inn, which at this time was situated on the east side of Preston Market-place. It was one of the higher-class social resorts. When the followers of the Old Pretender capitulated at Preston, on the 14th of November, 1715, the swords of the noblemen on his side were "delivered up at the Mitre inn." There is a tradition to the effect that in 1745 the Young Pretender stayed one night at the Mitre inn when either going south with his followers or retreating northwards with them. In the latter part of the century—probably about 1770—the present Mitre hotel, in Fishergate, became the successor of the old inn, which with adjoining property was cleared away in 1882-3 to make room for the site of the Harris Free Library building.

Ye 9th.—Some raine. Ye curate preach'd. I walk't to Enam with cousen T. Springham.

> The curate would be Mr. Farrand, stipendiary curate at the Parish Church.

LEVENS HALL *(Westmoriand).*

Owned and occupied from 1487 to 1688 by the Bellingham Family from Burneside Hall.

Ye 10th.—A wett day. I din'd att Penwortham, where we had a noble entertainment. There were Sr Tho Stanley and severall of this town, and Mrs Betty Banister, and ye widdow Tilsly with a sweet little boy, her sonne.

> The noble entertainment would be at Mr. Fleetwood's, Penwortham Hall.—Mrs. (old style for Miss) Betty Banister was no doubt Elizabeth, daughter of Alderman William Banister, who was Mayor of Preston in 1662-3.—Widow Tilsly, it is very likely, was the widow of Edward Tyldesley (son of Sir Thomas Tyldesley, the notable Royalist), of Tyldesley, Morleys, Myerscough Lodge, &c.

Ye 11th.—A fayr day. I was with my cousens most of ye day. Here was ye Ld Brandon. Great interest making for Parliament men. In ye evening I was with ye mayor and my cousens att Cuttlers, &c.

> Lord Brandon was Charles, son and heir of the Earl of Macclesfield. At Preston Guild, in 1682, he, his father, and a brother qualified as out-burgesses of the borough. He was a Colonel in the army and an Ambassador to Holland on the Royal succession. In 1701 he died and was buried in Westminster Abbey.—A general election was evidently supposed to be getting near, hence the "great interest making for Parliament men," i.e., members of Parliament; but such election did not take place till four months afterwards—January in the following year.—The Mayor was Alderman Nicholas Walmsley.—Cuttler was not at this time a local surname; so it is probable the visit was paid to either a person named Cuttler in the military entourage of the diarist or to some person or persons carrying on a cutlery business in the town.

Ye 12th.—Some raine in ye evening. This morning my cousens Springham went for Liverpoole. After dinner Coll and I walk't towards Walton and kill'd a hare.

> Coll. was Colonel Rawstorne.

Ye 13th.—Pretty fayr. We went a coursing. Din'd att Camell's, and was att night att Rigby's. One Southern, a German, came to us, who talk'd much of Jamaica.

> Camell may have been Thomas Camell, whose name appears in the list of those who paid the Hearth Tax at Preston in 1663, or a descendant of that person. If not, then, possibly Camell may be the form, as phonetically

spelt in 1688, at the time of the diarist, of the name Campbell; and, presuming this to be the case, then it is not unlikely that Camell was Thomas Campbell, who was made a freeman of Preston in 1662, renewed the privilege in 1682, subsequently went to live in Ashton-on-Ribble, which was then in what was called the "lower end of Preston," and quite an open country region suitable for coursing, and whilst residing there, in 1702, he again renewed his freedom.

Ye 14th.—A wett day. I was with the mayor and one Hollynhurst, the taylour, of London, att ye mitre, and after I treated ye master, and Gregson, and Cippax, att Tho. Bostocks.

 Hollynhurst was Thomas Hollinhurst, tailor, of London, and an in-burgess of Preston.—The master may have been the master of the Free School—the only public school in the town.—Gregson would be either Josiah Gregson, the Town Clerk and Clerk of the Recognisances, who was Mayor of Preston in 1693 and Guild Mayor in 1702, or his son Thomas, who was a glover.—Cippax or Kippax does not appear to have been a regular resident of Preston at this time. He may have been a descendant of a substantial family named Kippax, living at Preston in the early part of the century, and on a casual visit to the town.—Thomas Bostock was a local master barber, and would therefore, as business then went, be a person of some consequence. In 1694 he was elected a member of the Common Council of the borough, and held this position till his death in 1699.

Ye 15th.—Some raine. I was with Captain Cross. After with Mr. Parker and ye mayor. Sup't att cousen Patten's, and was sent for after by the mayor to waite on Sr Rich. Standish who will stand for burgess of Preston.

 Captain Cross was probably either Richard or Robert Cross, son of John Cross, yeoman, of Barton, near Preston.—Mr. Parker would be Edward Parker, son of Thomas Parker, Esq., of Browsholme Hall, before mentioned.—Sir Richard Standish was the younger son, and eventually the heir, of Thomas Standish, of Duxbury Hall, near Chorley, and, like his father, was a Colonel in the Parliamentary army. He represented' the county of Lancaster in the Parliament of 1656, and he was one of the Parliamentary representatives of Preston from 1658 to 1661. In February, 1676-77, he was created a baronet by Charles II—a dignity which became extinct with the third baronet, Sir F. Standish, in 1812.—The words " stand for Burgess of Preston " mean stand as a candidate for one of the Parliamentary seats here.

Ye 16th.—A fayr day.　We din'd att Mr. Hodgkinson's with Sr Thomas Stanley and others.　Mr Crossan preach'd in ye afternoon. Att evening we visited Cousen Patten.

> Mr. Crossan was, it is almost certain, Mr. Richard Croston, who took his degree of B.A. at Cambridge in 1674, was appointed Headmaster of Preston Grammar or Free School in 1680, subsequently took Holy Orders, was allowed by the Preston Common Council or Corporation, who had the control of the school named in their hands, to preach as well as teach, occasionally preached in the Preston Parish Church when the diarist was quartered in the town, and was amongst the non-jurors to King William III.

Ye 17th.—A very fayr day.　This morning there was a Councell held here about choosing burgesses for this place, and it was carry'd to elect Mr. Fleetwood and Sr Rich. Standish.　We walk'd in ye afternoon.　Was treated att Susans, and att night we went to see Lauc : Forth, of Kendall.

> The Corporation of Preston took a keen interest in politics at this time— even put forward, as they had previously done for many years, their own nominees for election as M.P.'s, and the " Councell " which was held was in all likelihood a meeting of the Common Council of the borough.—Mr. Fleetwood would be Mr. Edward Fleetwood, of Penwortham Hall.

Ye 18th.—Some light showers.　I was with Sr Rich. Standish and others.　We dranke hard att severall places.　My cousen Wm Bellingham came to town and Tim Bankes and his wife.

> William Bellingham was a son of James, and was younger brother of Alan Bellingham who sold Levens to Colonel Graham in 1686.—Bankes, as previously stated, was either from a country district in the neighbourhood of Levens or from the town of Kendal.

Ye 19th.—Some rain towards night.　I went with Coll. a setting, but had no luck.　This night I treated my Cousen Bellingham, Bankes, and Lau. Forth att ye miter.

> Going a setting would be either endeavouring to take birds with a setter dog or trying to get fish at a set, i.e., a place in a river where nets are fixed.　A fishery on the south or Penwortham side of the Ribble belonged to the Fleetwood family, of Penwortham Hall, and to this family " Coll "— Colonel Rawstorne—was related.

Ye 20th.—Some raine. I bowl'd with cousen W. B. Supt and lost money att cousen Patten's. Came late home, etc.

> W. B. was William Bellingham.—The money would, no doubt, be lost at card playing.

Ye 21th.—Very much raine. This afternoon I was with Mr. Franks, and treated him att Rattcliffs with Mr. Winkly.

> Mr. Franks would be Mr. John Francks, gentleman, of Preston.

Ye 22th.—A wett day. I was with Mr. G. Walmsley and others att Rigbys, and saw young mounsieur strike a woman, for which I struck him. I was after with W. B., Mr. Houghton, Mr. Ferrers, and others.

> Young mounsieur was Monsieur Brian. (See entry for December 31st, 1688, and January 11th, 1688-89.)—Mr. Ferrers would be either Mr. John Ferrars, a local gentleman, or one of his sons.

Ye 23th.—Much raine. We din'd att my cousen Patten's. We went to hear a quaker preach, but were disappointed.

Ye 24th.—A fayr day. We bowld. Mr. Rishton gave an account of the quaker. His name is Scansfield. He pretends to be a docter—a dangerous, seditious fellow, and not without some suspicion of being a jesuit. All his relations are R. C. He sayd there was a plott discovered of ye Bpps Keeping confederacy with Holland for raysing disturbances in England. He pretended to have an interest att Court, and to have an interest in electing Burgesses for this corporation. He and Tompson the Regulator were much together. Att night ye Coll. treated us att the anchor, where W. B. and Mr. Houghton, and D. Langton were very merry.

> Mr. Rishton may have been Alderman Ralph Rishton, or Wilfrid Rishton, the Mayor's Bailiff: if not, then probably Mr. Jeffrey Rishton, who took an interest in Church and municipal matters, eventually becoming a Church-warden and an Alderman of the Common Council.—The Quaker referred to was John Scansfield (called Scanfield by some persons and Scantfield by others). He is twice mentioned in Besse's " Sufferings " (vol 1, pp. 294 and 366) as among those imprisoned in London.—The letters R.C. of course

mean Roman Catholic.—Bpps is a contraction of Bishops.—A Regulator was one of a body appointed in 1687 to examine and revise the constitution and acts of various boroughs, "for the purpose of influencing the election of members of Parliament."—The Anchor was an inn at or near the top of Friargate, and in the immediate neighbourhood of the Market-place.—No D. Langton resided in Preston; and, unless the person mentioned by the diarist were on a visit to the town, the D must have been written in mistake for R. Richard Langton was at this time a member of the Council, and according to a subsequent entry in the diary, he seems to have lived in or had certain property near the Market-place. He was elected an Alderman in 1692, and was Mayor of the borough in 1692-3.

Ye 25th.—A very wett day. We had ye King's declaration for the farther assuring the rights of ye Church of England and for quieting elections for Parliament men. I walk'd with Coll, D. Chaddock, and W. Lemman to Penwortham, were we din'd, and call'd att the boat house with T. Fleetwood, and came home in good time.

Ye 26th.—Some raine. Here was a bull baiting. Ye bull broake loose and fell down Mr. Langton's cellar stayres, and broake open the doore, and had like to have killd 2 children and ye drawyer of ye anchor. We were with Mr. Kihnyon and Coll : att Rigby's.

The bull baiting was in the Market-place, at the south-west corner, where may still be seen the stone to which the bull ring was fastened.—The drawyer was the person employed to draw beer at the Anchor inn.—Mr. Kihnyon would most likely be Mr. Roger Kenyon, of Parkhead, near Blackburn, who was one of the M.P.'s for Clitheroe from 1690 to 1695.

Ye 27th.—A fayr day. I saw Mr. Chr Parker. I play'd with Cockshott at Mr. Chaddocks, and sup't att Cousen Johnson's.

Chr Parker was Christopher Parker, gent., of Bradkirk, near Kirkham, and Cockshott was either Jacob Cockshott, the Mayor's Bailiff in 1686-7, or John Cockshutt, gent., who was appointed Town Clerk of Preston in February 1693-4.

Ye 28th.—A fayr day. We had ye newes of ye Dutch designing to invade England with a great force of horse and foot and 60 sayle of ships to come into ye north.   I sup't att cousen Pattens.

Ye 29th.—A very wet afternoon.   I din'd wth ye Mayor, Sr Rich. Standish, Mr. Fleetwood, etc., att the Mitre, where Sr Rich. treated, and after at ye Anchor.

Ye 30th.—Some raine.   Mr. Gregory preach'd in ye afternoone.

Mr. Gregory would most likely be the Rev. Benjamin Gregory, who became an in-burgess of Preston in 1682, and some time between then and 1688 took Holy Orders.   The preaching would be at the Parish Church, and Mr. Gregory may have been the curate there or simply doing temporary clerical duty.

Octobr 01st.

Some raine.   I din'd wth ye Mayor at ye Serjeant's, and payd for my supper there.

At the Serjeant's means at the house of the Mayor's or the Town's Serjeant, each being a municipal official of considerable consequence.

Octbr ye 2d.—A fayr day. I went to Liverpoole. I mett T. Springham and T. Armitage, and had Dr. Richmond wth me att supper, and one Robinson, an impertinent surgeon, who came lately from Jamaica.

There was at this time a good deal of alarm, succeeded by a spirit of resistance, at Liverpool, in consequence of King James II having exercised certain power contained in a charter granted in 1685, and thereby removed from office Oliver Lyme, deputy mayor of Liverpool, and Silvester Richmond, a local magistrate.   Perhaps the unsettled state of affairs at Liverpool had induced the diarist to visit the place and make some inquiries on the subject.   The charter referred to, which rendered all the office-holders of the Corporation of Liverpool liable to be removed at the pleasure of the Crown, was supplanted by one granted by William III, in 1695.—Richmond is an old Liverpool name, and the Dr. mentioned may have been either Silvester Richmond, J.P., or a relation of that gentleman.

Ye 3d.—A fayr day.   I saw Sr Robert King in ye morning, and in ye afternoon I bowld wth him, and att night Mr. Richmond, Springham, Armitage, Norris, and I sate upp late.

> Norris was probably Thomas Norris, of Speke Hall, near Prescot, who was one of the members of Parliament for Liverpool from 1688 to 1694.

Ye 4th.—A fayr day.   I gott my freize from ye Custome house. Saw alderman Percivall, and Mr. Richmond.   Dranke too much Rum in ye morning.   Call'd att ormskirk on Will Patten.   Stayd att Rufford and came home before 6 a clock.

> Freize—a coarse woollen cloth or stuff, with a nap on one side.—Alderman Percivall was a member of the Liverpool Corporation.—Will Patten was a son of Alderman William Patten, of Preston.—Rufford is no doubt intended for Rufford Hall, near Ormskirk, the seat of the Hesketh family, and, when the diarist paid his visit, the residence of Thomas Hesketh.

Ye 5th.—A very wett day.   Mr. Winkly, ye new mayor, elected and sworn.   He took y oathes and subscribed against ye Solemn League and Covenant.   Ye bayliffes and serjeants swore likewise. We went with ye new mayor, where we were handsomely entertain'd. I went after to see Mr. Kennion, who shew'd me Ld Darby's letter, wherein was an account of ye K : Kindness to him and desires of his speedy coming to London.   This day and yesterday were ye quarter Sessions here : ye R. justices were not so haughty as formerly upon ye news of ye K : great civillity and condescension to ye R B of Canterbury and some other Bishops.   We have newes of ye restoring ye Charter of London and great Kindnesses to ye Church of Eng : and yt ye D of Ormond is to goe Ld Leivt of Ireland.

> The diarist had now got back to Preston.—The new Mayor was Alderman Thomas Winckley.—There were two Bailiffs, one being for the Mayor and the other for the town; the appointment of them took place annually; and different persons were usually selected each time.   There were also two Serjeants (the Mayor's and the town's), and their tenure of office was more stable or individually continuous than that of the Bailiffs.—The Mayor's entertainment would be in the Town Hall.—Mr. Kennion was, no doubt, the Mr. Kihnyon or Kenyon previously mentioned.—K : means King's.—R. refers to Romanist or Restoration justices—magistrates made

after Charles II had ascended the throne, and who would have an aversion to William III. Andrew Marvell, in a letter dated April 14th, 1670, and written when he was M.P. for Hull, says: "There is a new set of justices of peace framing through the whole Kingdom." These would, obviously, be magistrates of the Restoration period, and the bulk would, in religion, be Roman Catholics.—R B signifies Archbishop.—D obviously means Duke.—Ld Leivt is meant for Lord Lieutenant.

Ye 6th.—A fayr day. I din'd with ye Mayor at ye Bayliffes' feast, and was att night att Rigby's wth some company.

According to an old custom, the two Bailiffs at Preston had to provide yearly, at Easter, a feast for the Mayor, Corporation, burgesses, strangers, &c.; but the cost of this became so burdensome and the scenes which the feasting generated were so undesirable that the Corporation, in 1612, decided that the Bailiffs instead of paying for an Eastertide carousal should contribute annually £6 13s. 4d. apiece towards the salary of the Grammar School master (Preston Court Leet Records, p. 63). The feast referred to by the diarist would probably be one given on the occasion of the Mayor's election.

Ye 7th.—Some frost in ye morning and rain att night. I went to Penwortham, to Church, and din'd there. Came home in good time with Mr. Crosse.

The dining would be at Penwortham Hall, near the Church.—Mr. Crosse may have been a son of John Cross, yeoman, of Barton.

Ye 8th.—A very wett day. Ye Coll. and his Lady came to visit us. We went with them to Lawyer Pattens, and att night took 3 cans att Rigby's. Nanny fell ill.

Cans were vessels of various sizes, shapes, and materials, and were used for drinking wine, beer, &c.

Ye 9th.—A small frost. I had ye freize from Ireland. I receiv'd money for Betty, £7-10. Was att night att Rigby's, with Sr Edward Chisnell, Mr. Piggott, Leman, &c.

Sr Edward Chisnell was Sir Edward Chisenhall, who was knighted in 1671. He was a son of Edward Chisenhall, Esq., of Chisnell or Chisenhall Hall (now a farmhouse) in Coppull, near Chorley. In 1688-89 he was one of the Parliamentary representatives of Wigan, in the Whig interest.—Mr. Pigott would be either Mr. George Pigott, a Preston gentleman of very substantial position, or one of his sons—most likely Robert, who was the Mayor's Bailiff in 1684-85.—Leman was Alderman W. Lemon.

Ye 10th.—A wett day. I din'd att ye marsh, and att night was with Chisnell, Mr. Frankes, Coll., &c., att Rigby's. Nanny continues ill of a cold and feavour.

> The diarist would dine at the residence of the Swansea family, adjoining the west corner of Preston Marsh, that being the only house likely to have been at this time standing close to the waste or common ground mentioned. Chisnell was Sir Edward Chisenhall.

Ye 11th.—A fayr day. We had an account of ye P of O speech to ye States—that he went to reigne or dye ; if he reign'd he would be theyr friend ; if he dy'd he would dye theyr humble servant. This was in ye publick newes ler, as allso that there was written over Sir Wm Wm's door, " *Quos Jupiter vult perdere, hos dementat, si populus vult decipi decipiatur pro honore 7 Episcoporum O Fenestra !* " We visited ye old mayress, Mrs. Rigby, who was not well, and att night dranke 3 cans att Ratliffs.

> P of O was William Prince of Orange.—States, or rather States General, is the name given to the Legislature of the Netherlands Kingdom.— "Newes ler," i.e., news letter. Before the introduction of newspapers to the public, persons who wished for information on political matters employed writers to compose news letters which were circulated in manuscript form.—Sir Wm Wm's was Sir William Williams, who became Solicitor-General in the reign of James II., and was knighted. Macaulay says that " though in rank he [Williams] was only the second law officer of the Crown, his abilities, knowledge, and energy were such that he completely threw his superior into the shade."—Ratliff's would be George Ratcliffe's previously alluded to.

Ye 12th.—A fayr day. This is St. Wilfreds, att which time the new mayor enters into his office. The old mayor delivered him the staffe in the Church, and after some small compliments to each other we went to ye new mayor's to dinner, where we were very nobly entertain'd. I was ill of a cold and came home early.

> St. Wilfreds means the feast of St. Wilfrid.—The old Mayor, i.e., the Mayor for the municipal year 1687-8, which ended on October 5th, was Alderman Nicholas Walmsley; the new one, for 1688-9, being Alderman Thomas Winckley.—The staffe would be one of the two silver-headed

Mayoral wands, presented to the Preston Corporation respectively by
Edward Rigby, serjeant-at-law, for several years M.P., &c., for Preston,
and Thomas Sumner, Mayor of the borough in 1646-7.

Ye 13th.—A fayr day.   I tooke a vomitt of Cardus.   In the
afternoon I saw Mr. Chaddocke, who is newly come from Liverpoole.

> Cardus, i.e., Carduus Benedictus, or Blessed Thistle.   Mr. Matthew
> Robinson, M.D., in his herbal work says: "This plant is a native of
> warmer countries, and is raised with us in gardens," and that "an infusion
> of it, taken in large quantities, will excite vomiting."

Ye 14th.—A moyst day.   Ye mayor had a letter from Generll
Douglass.   My cold continues very violent.

> Probably the Generll here mentioned was General Douglas, who
> commanded the Scotch footguards, on the side of King William, at the
> battle of the Boyne in 1690.

Ye 15th.—Some raine.   Here came an express for ye Generall.

Ye 16th.—A fayr day.   We had newes that ye Dutch fleet were
seen of ye Dogger sands.   Here came Lord Mullineux and most of
R gentlemen of ye county.   They gave out Coms [commissions] :
ye old deputyes refused.   In ye afternoon I walk'd to Walton.   My
cold mends.

> Lord Mullineux was Caryl, third Viscount Molyneux, whom James II.
> made Lord Lieutenant and Custos-Rotulorum of the County of Lancaster,
> as well as Admiral of the narrow seas.   In the reign of the King just
> named Lord Mulyneux leased Fishwick Hall and demesnes, near Preston,
> for the lives and the use of three Benedictine monks.   He was outlawed by
> Parliament and precluded from compounding for his estates on account of
> his services in the cause of James II.; but subsequently, "by interest and
> paying an excessive fine," he was put into possession of his property.   He
> died at Croxteth, on February 2nd, 1698-9.—R gentlemen were of the
> Roman Catholic order.—Ye old Deputyes were County Deputy Lieutenants.

Ye 17th.—A fayr day.   Here came a party of Scotts of near
2000, which were parte of ye regiment of gaurds, Coll : Bochans
regiment and Coll Warchup's.   I saw Capt Coningham, Sr Albert's

ENTRANCE HALL, LEVENS,

Showing the Bellingham Stairway, and the Bellingham Coat of Arms in the ceiling.

sonne.   We had three Captaines quarter'd wth us—Deell, Carr, and Askyth—all very good men and Protestants.   I sate up late and dranke hard with them.

Ye 18th.—A fayr day.   I was very ill all this day with last night's debauch.   I had severall friendes came to visitt me.

Ye 19th.—A fayr day.   I had letters and a bill from home of £122, which I sent that day to Liverpoole.   I play'd with Mr. Frankes att his own house this evening.

> The diarist's home was at Gernonstown, now Castlebellingham.

Ye 20th.—A very wett day.   I tooke Physick, wch wrought well.   Mr. Hodgkinson came to sit wth me.

> Mr. Hodgkinson was Alderman Thomas Hodgkinson.

Ye 21th.—Much raine last night.   This day brought the newes of the E. of Darby's being made Ld Lewt of Cheshire and Lancashire, for which ye bells rung most of ye day.   I was ill and went not to church in ye morning.

> William George Richard Stanley, 9th Earl of Derby, was made Lord Lieutenant of Lancashire in 1676; some time after James II. came to the throne he was removed from that position; but on October 17th, 1688, he was reinstated and simultaneously made Lord Lieutenant of Cheshire. A branch of the house of Stanley had just become connected by marriage with a Preston family—on August 16th, 1688, Elizabeth, only daughter and heiress of Thomas Patten, son of Alderman William Patten, of Preston, was married to Sir Thomas Stanley, of Bickerstaffe, fourth baronet, whilst a prospective candidate for one of Preston's Parliamentary seats, at the next election, was apparently the Hon. James Stanley, brother of the Earl before mentioned (the election took place in about three months, and the Hon. James Stanley was made M.P., his colleague being Thomas Patten)— hence the ringing of the church bells on the receipt of the news that honours had been conferred on Lord Derby.

Ye 22th.—Much raine last night.   I tooke Physick, and am much better of my cold. Here came some Irish foot of Hamilton's.

> Richard Hamilton was appointed Brigadier-General in the Irish army. "When the Dutch invasion was expected, he came across Saint George's

Channel with the troops which Tyrconnel sent to reinforce the royal army."
(Macaulay's History of England.)   The soldiers referred to by the
diarist were probably some infantry temporarily detached from those under
Hamilton's command.

Ye 23th.—A wett day.   No newes of the Dutch.   Ye Irish
marched away.   They belonged to [? were in charge of] one Mc
Guire and Rolston.   I sup't att Coll. Rawstorn's.

Ye 24th.—A very wett day.   I sup't att Mr. Hodgkinson's.

Ye 25th.—Some raine.   Mr. Gregson and I walk't to Walton,
and att night was att ye Talbott wth Chaddock, Dr., Lemmin, and
others.

> Dr. would be Dr. Lee.

Ye 26th.—A fayr day.   This afternoon ye fayr was proclaimd,
and we were treated by the bayliffs.

> This fair was a very old one—it was established by a Charter of Edward
> III.—and lasted a week.

Ye 27th.—Very violent raine and hayl.   Att night I was wth
Sr Edward Chisnell, Mr. Fleetwood, and Coll, att anchor.   I layd a
bottle of sack wth Dr. Lee that ye sige before Phillipbourgh was
raysed before this day.   Wm. Belling[ham] and Mr. Hilton came
to town, etc.

> Phillipbourgh, i.e., Philippsburg, a town of Baden, on the right bank of
> the Rhine, and about 15 miles from Carlsruhe, was often besieged.   It was
> twice taken by the French in the Thirty Years war, was again taken by
> them in 1688 as well as in 1734, and in 1800, after it had been once more
> taken by the French, its fortifications were demolished.—When the diarist
> made this entry there were several persons named Hilton, chiefly on the
> out-burgess list of Preston, who lived in the Brindle district, near Chorley,
> and the Mr. Hilton mentioned may have been one of them.

Ye 28th.—Some raine.   I supt att cousen Patten's wth W. B.

> W.B.—William Bellingham.

Ye 29th.—Indifferent fayr. I was wth W. B. and others att Bostocks. I layd £5 wth Dr. Worton yt Phillipbourg would not be taken. Mr. Houghton and Wm. Patten had this night a great quarrell att Turlagh's, and blowes given.

Ye 30th.—A fayr day. W. B. went for London. I sent 6 guinnyes by him to my sister. There passed a challenge between Wim Patten and Mr. Houghton, but mett not.

W. B. would probably be William Bellingham, barrister.

Ye 31th.—A fayr day. I went early this morning to Walton, where I found Mr. Houghton ready to come forth to meet Wm. Patten, who wrote to him ye night before. I disposed him for a reconciliation, and he came to town. I brought Patten to Tirlaghs, and fully reconcil'd them. We mett againe att night, and dranke a bottle. We had an account from Yorkshire that guns were heard [and a] meter seen.

Tirlagh's is intended for Turlagh's, a name which has been previously explained.—Meter means meteor.

Novembr ye 1st, 1688.

A very fayr day. It being my birth[day] I treated some freindes, and att night was in Mr. Piggotts room. I gave Mr. Hebson halfe a crown, to receive 4 for it if ye Dutch invaded us before twelfth day next.

Mr. Hebson was Mr. William Hebson, a member of the Common Council of Preston. The diarist won his bet, as William, Prince of Orange, landed on November 5th.

Ye 2d.—A fayr day. I walk'd on ye moore in ye morning.

Ye moore—Preston Moor, on the north side of the town.

Ye 3d. A fayr day, but high wind. Att E[ast]. I Tooke Physik which wrought very kindly.

Ye 4th.—A fayr day : high E wind. Ye H : Eu : [Holy Eucharist] was celebrated, and I received. Mr. Hodgkinson, Deputy Mayor.

Ye 5th.—A moyst day. Mr. Piggott and I walk'd to Walton. The anniversary was kept there wth much modesty—prayers, ringing of bells, and few bonefires.

> This was the Gunpowder Plot anniversary.

Ye 6th.—A fayr day. I had an account of ye Dutch being seen between Dover and Callis, on Saturday last att one a clock, steering towards ye west of England. This day I assigned my bill wth Mr. Wm. Clayton, and receiv'd £20 of him in money and £30 on demaund, and from Mr. Cottam a noates [notice] from Mr. Clayton of £30 on demaund, and from Cottham for £40 payable within 10 dayes. I was great parte of ye afternoone wth Mr. Swetman [and] Mr. Wamsly.

> Mr. William Clayton was a son of Mr. Robert Clayton, gent., of Fulwood. Dr. Clayton, a Roman Catholic prelate (successively Bishop of Killala, Cork, and Clogher), Lord Chief Justice Clayton of the Common Pleas, Ireland, and Sir Richard Clayton, Bart., F.S.A. (a nephew of the latter), were descendants of or connected with the Clayton family of Fulwood.—Mr. Cottam was Mr. William Cottam, a member of Preston Common Council, and the Cottham mentioned was evidently the same person.—Mr. Swetman was not a resident of Preston. The name may be intended for Swettenham, or Sweetman, or Swetnam. Fleetwood, in his diary, refers to a George Swetnam.

Ye 7th.—A moyst day. Betty was not well. We eat oysters att ye anchor, which came fresh from London.

Ye 8th.—A fayr day. Mr. Chaddock, Mr. Franks, and I walk'd to Penwortham, and din'd there, and call'd att ye boat house wth Mr. Fleetwood and Dr. Lee.

Ye 9th.—A wett day.   We receiv'd ye newes of ye Dutch landing att Dartmouth, Torbay, and Exmouth, in ye west of England, on Monday last, etc.

> This news was quite correct. The Dutch troops of William Prince of Orange disembarked at Torbay on Monday the fifth of November.

Ye 10th.—A fayr but cloudy day.   In ye afternoone I was wth Mr. Fleetwood, Mr. Osberston, and others att Bostock's, Mitre, and Rattliffes.   I mett a hott man att ye coffee house who inveigh'd bitterly against ye P : of O.

> Osberston does not appear in any of the contemporary local name lists. Perhaps it is a variant of or intended for Osbaldeston; there being at this time persons bearing such name in both Preston and a rural district on the east side of the town.—A hott man: One excited, fierce, or passionate.— P of O: Prince of Orange.

Ye 11th.—A fayr day.   We had ye newes of ye Dutch confirm'd, and that they were gone to Exeter.   Mr. Chaddock receiv'd a letter from an unknown hand wth much private newes in it.

Ye 12th.—A frost.   I walk'd wth Mr. Chaddock to Camell's. I play'd and won some money att tables.   Att night I was wth some freindes att Rigby's, and Mrs. Chaddock came in to complaine, etc.

Ye 13th.—A hard frost.   Ye bagg of Preston was forgotten at Knutsford, but came in about 5 in ye evening, and brought an account of yt ye P. of O. was possesst of Exeter, and had above 20,000 strong.   There [is] some [rumour or talk] of accommodation.   Mr. Chaddock receiv'd another letter from ye unknown hand.   I din'd wth Mr. Franks.   Mr. Rycroft dyed suddinly this morning.

> Ye bagg would be the mail bag.—Mr. Rycroft was the Rev. Henry Rycroft, of Penwortham.

Ye 14th.—A very hard frost. I walk'd wth ye Coll. to Penwortham, and din'd there, and was att the funerall of Mr. Rycroft, and came home early.

Ye 15th.—The frost thawen. Severall of ye town went to ye funerall of Sr Tho. Clifton's only sonne ; and Robert Rigby's wife was buryed here. I was with Mr. Wamsly, who preach'd a very ingenious funerall sermon.

Sir Thomas Clifton resided at Lytham Hall. His only son, named Thomas, was but 20 years of age at the time of his death, and he was interred in the south aisle of Kirkham Parish Church. At this time Lytham Hall was a comparatively small building. Portions of the contiguous grounds were laid out in the Dutch style. Between 1757 and 1764 a great addition was made to the hall; and it included much internal embellishment, the chief ceilings being decorated by Italian workmen. The brickwork of the building is the most perfect of any to be met with in this part of the country. The entire cost of the extension was about £80,000. The park connected with Lytham Hall was something like 100 acres in area when the building was enlarged: between 1845 and 1860 it was increased to about 600 acres, under the management of the late Mr. James Fair, the very able and much respected estate agent of the Clifton family. For many years the present heir to the Clifton property (John Talbot Clifton, Esq.) did not occupy the hall—much of his time being taken up in travelling; but on the 14th of February, 1908, he came to reside at the ancestral mansion, along with Mrs. Clifton, his wife; and their home-coming caused much local gladness and rejoicing.—The person whose wife's burial is referred to was either Robert Rigby, draper, of Preston, or Robert, son of Edward Rigby, merchant tailor, of London.— The preacher named would in all likelihood be the Rev. George Walmsley, of Preston.

Ye 16th.—A dry day. Severall of ye town went to meet ye Curate, who brought home his wife. Ye newes was that severall had gone to ye K[ing]. Att night I was wth Lewt Stanly, and after wth Mr. Rishton, Hornby, and Wamsly, a parson, about R. Rishton's poast office affayer.

The curate was Mr. Farrand.—Lewt (Lieutenant) Stanley would be the Hon. Robert Stanley, brother of the Earl of Derby.—Hornby was probably Edmund, son of Geoffrey Hornby, of Poulton-le-Fylde. He married a daughter of Geoffrey Rishton, of Antley Hall, near Accrington, M.P. for Preston 1661-67. One of his (Edmund's) descendants, the Rev. Geoffrey

Hornby, D.D., Rector of Winwick, married Lucy, sister of Edward 12th Earl of Derby.—Ralph Rishton (an Alderman of the Council) was at this time, or had been shortly before, deputy postmaster of Preston; but in conducting the business he sustained a very serious pecuniary loss, and he sent a petition to the Treasury Lords, in which he stated that "for many years he provided horses and despatched the packets between Wigan and Kendal, which is a hundred north country miles, forwards and backwards, for a salary of only £70 per annum, and also found horses and despatched packets from Wigan to Lancaster, which is sixty-eight long miles, for a salary of £50 per annum, spending his whole time with the two services; and though your petitioner begun with a considerable fortune, he is now penniless and beggared, and dismissed the office because he is in arrears," and he "prays that his debts may be remitted and that the Postmaster-General may not be permitted 'to pursue him and put him in prison.'" (Lewins's Her Majesty's Mails, p. 62.)

Ye 17th.—Some frost and very dry. I was wth Mr. Rishton's freindes. After I was wth Mr. Fleetwood and others, and we had an account given by Mr. Stanly, Clifton, and Laban that the Ld Delamare was risen and gathering men att Manchester; and about 9 att night we had it confirm'd by one Hugh Gorny, a carrier who goes from this town to Manchester, who sayd that he saw ye Lord himselfe att ye head of 60 horse, and that it was reported that severall of the town would rise wth him.

This was Henry the second Lord Delamere. In 1685 he was committed to the Tower, and afterwards charged, at the bar of the House of Lords, with conspiracy, along with Charles Gerrard, Esq., and others, "to dethrone His Majesty James II., with assembling to make war in the County of Chester, and with a desire to seize the city of Chester and the castle of the said city." The evidence given against him was worthless, and the peers before whom he was tried unanimously decided that he was not guilty. In 1688, on the arrival of the Prince of Orange in Enlgand, Lord Delamere "raised a considerable force in Cheshire and Lancashire in support of the Revolution, and his lordship, accompanied by the Marquis of Halifax and the Earl of Shrewsbury, was the bearer of a message to James II. requiring him to quit his palace and abdicate his throne."

Ye 18th.—A very cold, dry day. Our newes that ye Ld Lovelace was apprehended att Ceirencester wth 13 more, after having made a sharp resistance and killed major Loveage and his

sonne of ye militia, yt severall gen : [gentlemen] are joyn'd Ld
Delamere, and yt he designs for Yorkshire.   I was wth Coll :
and Capt. Greene att Mitton's.

> Captain Greene was presumably a Militia officer.—Mitton's would be
> John Mitton's, Preston.   He was evidently an innkeeper.

Ye 19th.—A frost and much snow.   Nabby was not well.   I
was wth Coll:, Capt. Greene, mr. mayor, etc., att Cowper's

Ye 20th.—A great thaw.   We had an account of Ld Cornburyes
revolt wth 3 Regements of horse and dragoons to ye P. of O.   I
was att night wth Coll : and severall others in ye weend, etc.

> The nobleman mentioned was Edward Viscount Cornbrook, eldest son
> of the Earl of Clarendon.   He took the three regiments from Salisbury, in
> a south-western direction.   When between Dorchester and Axminster some
> of the officers became suspicious, and as Cornbrook could not, when asked,
> produce his orders justifying the movements, the bulk of the troops
> returned to Salisbury.—The weend would be Main Sprit Weind in Preston
> (between Fishergate and Church-street, on the south side), in which used
> to reside gentlemen of much municipal consequence.

Ye 21th.—Much snow and then a thaw.   Ye Earl of Derby
came to this town about 12 of ye clock.   He was wth ye militia
officers that afternoon.   Att night he was treated by the mayor att
Mr. Hodghkinson's.   I sup't there and sate up till 5 in ye morning.   Some justices were sworn, but Mr. Bradill refus'd.   An
express came to my Ld about 2 to suppress ye Ld Delamere.

> Mr. Bradill was Mr. Thomas Braddyll, of Portfield House, near Whalley—
> a mansion pulled down in the 18th century.   At the time when the entry in
> the diary was made he owned Samlesbury Old Hall, &c., near Preston.
> The Braddylls of Conishead Priory, near Ulverston, were representatives of
> his family.

Ye 22th.—A very wett day.   My Lord dind and was accom-
pany'd by severall towards Wiggan.   I was ill wth sitting upp
so late.

Ye 23th.—Some wett this morning.   Here came an express from ye Lord Darby to Coll Rawstorne to bring all the Regiment to Wiggan, that his Lordship had receiv'd information that there were designes against his life, and that some men were sent to apprehend him, and therefore commanded all the help imaginable to come to secure his person.   I was lett blood this day for the paine in my shoulder which was very violent.   Att night I was wth Sr Chr Phillipson and his brother att the Anchor, and G. Foxcroft, Mr. Fletcher, and R. Rishton.

> There does not appear to have been any one named Foxcroft residing in Preston or the neighbourhood when the diarist was quartered in the town; but there were two or three persons respectively named George Foxcroft at Lancaster, and possibly the G. Foxcroft mentioned was one of them. —William Fletcher, a Preston tradesman, may have been the Mr. Fletcher alluded to.—R. Rishton would be the unfortunate deputy postmaster previously mentioned.

Ye 24th.—A fayr day.   My paine increases.   I was for some time wth Mr. Fleetwood and others att Cowpers and ye mitre.

Ye 25th.—A very wett day.   I sweat and was visited in ye evening by ye mayor and severall others.   I this [day] received ye R. decl. from C. F. and shewed it ye mayor.   A stranger preach'd.

> Alderman Thomas Winckley was the Mayor.—R. decl., i.e., Royal declaration.

Ye 26th.—A fayr day.   Capt. Piggott's and Rigby's companyes drew upp in ye Market Place.   I was att Rigby's wth Dr Lee and others, and sup't and playd att cards att my cousen Johnson's.

Ye 27th.—A frost.   We had an account of Yorke being seized by Lord Danby, Dunblane, Fairfax, &c., and yt ye militia had joyn'd them.   I was att night wth ye mayor, Capt. Rigby, G. Rigby, and others.

> York was seized on November 22nd by the Earl of Danby.   He was at the head of about 100 horse soldiers: the militia in the city immediately sided with him, and the garrison was speedily disarmed.—Lord Dunblane was

the heir apparent to the Danby earldom.—Fairfax would be the 5th Earl.—
It is very probable that Captain Rigby was Thomas, eldest son of
Lieut.-Colonel Rigby, who was a son of the notable Colonel Rigby, of
Middleton, in Goosnargh, near Preston.—G. Rigby was Gilbert Rigby,
brother of Thomas.

Ye 28th.—A frost. I din'd att Camells wth Mr. Fleetwood,
Parker, and severall others, and att night was wth Mr. Rich.
Percivall, of Manchester, etc.

Ye 29th.—A frost. We had an account of ye desertion of
Prince George, D of Ormond and Grafton, Lds Churchill, Arran,
Coll. Berkeley, and severall others. I sup't att ye Mitre wth Dr.
Lee, Mr. Lemman, Greefeild, etc.

> The desertion to the side of the Prince of Orange of Prince George
> (son-in-law of James II), the Dukes of Ormonde, Grafton, &c., took place
> on or about the 25th of November.—Mr. Lemman was Alderman Lemon.—
> Greefeild was Christopher Greenfield, who practised as a lawyer in Preston
> for some time, married a daughter of Dr. Bushell, vicar of Preston, was
> one of the members of Parliament for Preston from March 1689-90 to
> November 1695, and was knighted whilst M.P.

Ye 30th.—A frost. Dean Ward was here. He tould me of ye
discorse between Dr Owens and one Lancaster, att Prescott, about
ye birth of ye P. of W, wch a woman overheard, and that it was a
sham and nothing more.

> A statement had been made public to the effect that Mary, Queen of
> James II, was confined on June 10th, and had given birth on that day to a
> prince—the Prince of Wales; but "the nation over which, according to the
> ordinary course of succession, he would have reigned was fully persuaded
> that the mother was not really pregnant." (Macaulay's History of
> England.) This view of the case was, however, incorrect: there was born
> on the day named "the most unfortunate of princes, destined to seventy-
> seven years of exile and wandering, of vain projects, of honours more
> galling than insults, and of hopes such as make the heart sick." (Ibid.)
> This prince was the one now historically known as the "Old Pretender."

SMALL DRAWING ROOM, LEVENS,

Containing Carved Oak Chimney Piece, centrally surmounted with Bellingham Arms, &c.

Dec. ye 1st.

A fayr day, but cold. My paine in ye shoulder continues, for which I sweat; and att evening I treated cousens Johnson and Patten wth oysters and wine, and playd att Cards pretty late.

Ye 2nd.—A dry, cold day. I was not att church in ye morning, but heard yt ye vicar preach'd a very factious sermon. Ye curate made a good serm: in ye afternoon.

> The Rev. Thomas Birch was the vicar, and Mr. Farrand was the curate.

Ye 3d.—A dry, cold day. I tooke Physick for my paine, which continues very violent. In ye evening my cousens Johnson and Patten came, and sate wth me and play'd cards till it was late.

Ye 4th.—A cold, dry day. We had an account of Bristoll, Plymouth, Hull, Newcastle, Carlisle, and severall other places sur-rendred for ye P of O. Proclamations for a Parliament to sitt ye 15th of January. I wrote severall letters for Ireland. Was wth ye Rigbys. Ye Capt Challenged Capt Brathwait who recanted.

> The first mentioned officer was, presumably Captain Rigby, and the second Captain Thomas Braithwaite.

Ye 5th.—A cold, dry day. In ye afternoon I walk'd wth Collonel to Penwortham. Was wth Mr. Greenfeild and others att Rigbys. Supt at Cousen Pattens, and playd att cards.

Ye 6th.—A frost. I walk'd wth Mr. Chaddock and Franks to the Marsh. Was wth Mr. Kennyon att Coopers, and after wth Mr. Farrington ye parson att Rigby's.

Ye 7th.—A fayr frost. We had an account of an address from ye navy, and that our fleet and ye Dutch lay very freindly together att Portsmouth. I was att evening wth Mr. Mayor and severall others att Rigbys.

Ye 8th.—A frost. I was wth Mr. Fleetwood and parted early. Dr. Lee tould ye story of ye lightning killing 2 men in ye middle of 12 or 13, and took such serpentine motions, and went out of ye top of ye house.

Ye 9th.—A fayr day. I walk'd to Penwortham, and heard Mr. Gregory, and din'd there, and was att Ratcliffe's, wth Mr. Greenfeild and others, where ye P : O. De was read, etc.

> The diarist would hear Mr. (the Rev. Benjamin) Gregory read the service, or preach, in Penwortham Parish Church.—The De. (Declaration) was perhaps that issued at the Hague, by the Prince of Orange, on October 10th, 1688, and, later, translated and condensed by Gilbert (afterwards Bishop) Burnet, and then circulated in England—a Declaration in which the Prince of Orange referred to the illegal acts of James II, his father-in-law, accepted the invitation of the English Parliament to take the place of James on the throne, and proclaim " a free and legal parliament," &c. ; or it may have been the " Supplementary Declaration " that was circulated —a Declaration which included a fierce attack on Roman Catholics, causing much excitement in the country, and which, many years afterwards, turned out to have been a forgery by Hugh Speke.

Ye 10th.—A fayr day. I sweat. Ye soldiers went to Physick chappell and tooke downe ye Bell, &c.

> There seems to be a mistake or some omission of details here. Dom. Gregory (Bartholomew Hesketh, who belonged to a family in Goosnargh, near Preston) built a Roman Catholic chapel at or near Fishwick Hall, on the east side of Preston, and had charge of the mission there. " The chapel had an organ, a pulpit, and two bells ; but, on the termination of the respite from persecution which Catholics enjoyed during the short reign of James II, the bells were buried near the stable wall adjoining the Hall. They were afterwards removed to the cellar of the White Bull Inn, near the Parish Church, in Preston, and at that time kept by a Catholic, Richard Jackson, who rented a portion of the Fishwick estate." (Hewitson's History of Preston, p. 387.) In Fishwick's History of the Parish of Preston, p. 306, there is reproduced some evidence taken from the " informations " in the forfeited estate papers, at the Public Record Office, which fully confirms this statement.

Ye 11th.—A wett day. I went to ye boat house, to see a match att shooting between one Brown of Yorkshire and Billington of Lancashire. They shott but halfe of a sett. I sup't att Cousen

Patten's. We had account of severall vessells arriv'd att Liverpoole, yesterday, wth multitudes of English who fled out of Ireland for fear of a massacre.

Ye 12th.—A moyst day. We heard the boyes declaime att school. I went to see the shooting att boat house. Was wth Dr. Lee, Mr. Chaddock, and others att George Rattliffes. Tooke a long farewell. B was tould ye account of ye Lord of Meath's going to Tirconnell and desiring armes for theyr protection, but was refus'd and threatned and charg'd wth Rebellion.

> Tirconnell was Richard Talbot, Earl of Tyrconnel, the General of the soldiers of James II in Ireland.

Ye 13th.—A very wett day. I rode to Camells to see ye ship wch came from Holland. Ye master tould me he was 3 weekes since att Ireland, and ye Custome house officer assur'd him there were armes lately come over for 15,000 men. He saw 2 dutch ships off Pyle of fother. Dean Ward came from Liverpoole, and confirms the account of 500 being come from Ireland for fear of a massacre, thatt Ld of Meath and Granard went to Tirconnell who gave them no satisfaction, and that he believ'd Ld Meath was come over to the P of O, and yt ye D of Orm was gone into Ireland wth a considerable force.

> The Pyle of fother, i.e., the Pile of Fouldrey, is a flat island, with an area of 19 acres, near the mouth of Walney Channel, and about three miles south-east of Barrow-in-Furness. There are on it the ruins of a castle which was built in the time of King Stephen.—The Duke of Ormond was now definitely on the side of the Prince of Orange.

Ye 14th.—A moyst day. We had an acct [account] of ye K, Q, and P [King, Queen, and Prince] being withdrawn towards Ireland. I was wth Sr. Rich. Standish, major Farrington, &c.

> Major Farrington would be either Henry or William Farington, of Worden Hall, Leyland.

Ye 15th.—A fayr day.   We had an account by express this morning, from Wiggan, that 8,000 Scotch and Irish were ravaging the Kingdom, yt they massacred in Breimingham, burnt Stafford, and were moving towards Newcastle [? under-Lyme], upon which this town was making all speedy preparation and sent severall expresses.   I was desir'd to take care of the horse, wch I did, and gott severall who were very ready but wanted arms.   We searcht severall suspected houses, but found very little.   We return'd about 4 a clock, mett ye mayor, and I entred.   About 50 gave theyr names to serve in ye horse.

> The ravaging Scotch and Irish would be soldiers on the side of James II.—The entries were made on behalf of the Prince of Orange.

Ye 16th.—A fayr day.   I had above 60 who rode under my command.   I march'd to ye mill hill, where I exercized them, and brought them into ye town, where they gave 2 very good volleys. I treated ym.   Mr. Clarett this day brought an account of the K being stoppt att Feversham, of the Chancellor and others being taken.   A letter came from my Ld Derby confirming the newes of the Irish and Scotch.   Mr. Rishton came from Warrington.   I was wth Captaine Bold.

> Mill Hill was in a field on the eastern side of Preston—between the present Park-road and Deepdale-road.—Mr. Clarett was not a local person. —The King (James II) was caught at Emley Ferry, near the Isle of Sheppey, not far from Faversham, whilst on a hoy, waiting to make his escape to the Continent.   Eventually, after being at Rochester for a time, he returned, of his own accord, to London.—The Chancellor (Lord Chancellor Jeffreys) was caught at Wapping, disguised as a sailor, and removed to the Tower of London, where he died.—Captain Bold, it is almost a certainty, was Peter Bold, Knight of the Shire (Lancashire) in 1677, and High Sheriff of the county in 1690.

Ye 17th.—A wett day.   I drew out ye Volunteers, who appear'd better appointed than yesterday.   We exercised on ye marsh, and they performed admirably.   We marcht in a full body through the town, gave a volley, and dismiss'd.   We had 2 expresses, one from ye Lord Danby, from York, wh brought an account yt he was advanceing wth 2 Regiments of foot, 8 troop of horse, and one of grenadiers ; ye other from Coll Rawstorne, that the Irish were dispers'd about [? Shrew]sbury, and had layd down theyr arms. Sr Tho Clifton was taken and brother.

Ye 18th.—A wett day.   I drew out ye troop, but ye raine drove us in againe.   We had a report of ye King's death [James II], but, God be prays'd, it prov'd false.   The newes sayes that Tirconnell was seiz'd, together wth ye castle of Dublin, by Lords Granard, Meath, Mou[nt]joy, and Inchequin.   I was wth parte of ye troop, who treated me att ye anchor, and after wth Coll Rigby, Capt Bold, &c.

> Coll Rigby was Lieutenant-Colonel Rigby, who served under his father (Colonel Rigby, ob. 1650) in the Parliamentary army.

Ye 19th.—A frost.   Ye militia Companyes and troop drew out. I saw them exercise very ill.   I was after wth ye mayor, Capt Bold, and others att ye Dogg, and after att ye Mitre.   Ye mayor receiv'd a fresh account from Lancaster, which came from Kendall, that ye Scotch and Irish were gone Yorkshire road and had burnt Halifax ; but it is not believ'd.   Ye mayor shewed me ye letter at ten at night.

> Ye Dogg was the name of a Preston inn ; and probably the present Old Dog Inn, on the south side of Church-street, if it be not the actual building, occupies the same site.

Ye 20th.—A great frost.   I walk'd wth Dr Lee, Mr. Lemman, and Mr Langton to Penwortham, where we were nobly entertain'd. I won some money.   Capt Bold came after dinner and was much in drinke.   Att night I was wth the mayor, att [? had] ale, &c.

> The place where the party were entertained at was Penwortham Hall.— Mr. Langton would be Mr. Richard Langton, a member of the Preston Common Council.

Ye 21th.—A hard frost. Our newes yt ye K [King] had againe retir'd to Rochester, yt P [Prince of Orange] come to St. James. I wrote severall letters to Ireland, and was att Mr. Rigbys [with] Capt Bold, Mr. Fleetwood, and others.

Ye 22nd.—A hard frost. Tom White came here. I gott him a pass from the mayor, gave him £5, and sent him towards Kirkham. I was wth Mr. Fleetwood, Mr. Sherburn of Stanihurst, and others, att ye mitre, and after wth Kellett att ye White bull.

> White was not a Preston person.—Mr. Sherburn was Mr. Richard Sherburn, of Stonyhurst, his ancestral home, a few miles north-west of Whalley. For many years it has been a Roman Catholic College, belonging to the Order of Jesuits, and it stands high in the domains of education.

Ye 23th.—A great frost. We had little newes, but that there would be great alterations in Ireland, and its doubted whether ye King will leave ye Kingdome. We walk'd in ye afternoon, and miss'd a railing sermon wch ye Vicar Preached against ye ceremonyes of ye Church.

Ye 24th.—A great frost. Ribble was frozen over. Mr. Gregson and I went a gunning, but gott little, only some few small birds. Capt Bold went hence. We din'd att Dr Lees. Was wth Capt Clayton and his sonne att Mittons. He brought an Irish proclamation wth him, which was sent to Liverpoole, by order of Tirconnell, to ye mayor.

> Captain Clayton would be a member of or connected with the Clayton family of Fulwood.

Ye 25th.—A gentle thaw. Little newes. Ye K: continues still att Rochester. Debates about a free Parliament. Tirconnell refuses to surrender Ireland. I was wth Sr Tho Stanly and much company at Serjeant Wall's.

> Anthony Wall, gent., had this year been elected sub-Bailiff or Town's Serjeant.

Ye 26th.—A hard frost.   We were nobly entertained att ye mayors.   Went after to one of ye Serjeants ; so to Mittons ; and from thence to play att ye Coffee house, where we won £30.

One of ye Serjeants, i.e., either the Mayor's or the town's Serjeant.—The Coffee house probably adjoined a place called the Coffee Garden, which was on the east side of Main Sprit Weind.

Ye 27th.—A hard frost.   Dr Lee went from hence to Fullwood under halfe an houre for a wager.   I din'd wth much company att Mr. Rigby's ; but a very ill dinner.   After waited on ye Mayor ; to the other Serjeants [house] ; from thence to Rattcliffe's ; and so to play, to ye Coffee house, where I lost £20, and Mr. Greenfeild was halfes and mett a disappointment.

Fulwood, at its nearest boundary line, is only a mile and a half from Preston Town Hall ; so that if Dr. Lee made a bet of the kind named he must, supposing he walked and was not in any way handicapped by infirmity, have either started at some point in Preston farther south than the Town Hall—the usual place for calculating distances to and from the borough—or finished in some part of Fulwood more remote than the boundary line mentioned.

Ye 28th.—A hard frost.   We had an account of ye King's being gone towards France.   I sent T. White away wth some letters.   I was wth Mr. Mayor and Chr Parker att Cravens, and after sup't att Cousen Johnson's.

Cravens was Mr. Edward Craven's.

Ye 29th.—A frost.   Mr. Fleetwood came hither, and seemes unwilling to stand for Parliament man.   I was wth him att ye Dogg.   Mr. Hodgkinson, Mrs Langton, and her sister sup't wth us.

Mr. Fleetwood was Edward, son of Mr. John Fleetwood, of Penwortham.— Mr. Hodgkinson was Alderman Thomas Hodgkinson, of Preston.—Mrs. Langton was the wife of Richard Langton, a member of the Council, and in 1692-3 Mayor of Preston. Her maiden name was Mary Hodgkinson : she was the only daughter of William Hodgkinson, of Preston, gent., and niece of Alderman Thomas Hodgkinson before mentioned.

Ye 30th.—A hard frost. I walk't after dinner to Penwortham, over ye ice, wth Mr. Franks, and saw severall people sliding and walking over Ribble.

Ye 31th.—A hard frost. Cousen Johnson, Bryan, and I walk't 8 miles a fowling, and mett nothing. We sup't att Cousen Patten's, and came late home. I was invited to Mr. Franks, but it was after dinner.

Januar. ye 1st [1688-89].

A very hard frost. A noble entertainment att Penwortham. I receiv'd bad newes from Ireland, of great preparations by Tirconnell, and that T. White was afraid of possession being taken. T. White return'd from Liverpoole, but I sent him again wth more letters, etc.

The entertainment would, as usual, be at Penwortham Hall.

Ye 2d.—A very hard frost. I saw Mr. Sympson, of Kendall, and treated him. We sup't att cousen Johnson's wth Mr. Rigby and his Lady, etc.

Ye 3rd.—Much snow. I had my cousens and Mr. Sympson and wife to supper. We were very merry, and made ye discovery of cous[en] Johnson's love letter-writing to 2 Ladyes. I saw R P and O.

The initials probably refer to Rigby, Patten, and Osberston or Osbaldeston.

Ye 4th.—A frost continues. I walk't to Walton. Poast came in late. I reproachd. Was wth ye mayor att widdow Clifton's, eating of oysters which came from London.

Widow Clifton was probably a local innkeeper.

Ye 5th.—A hard frost. We din'd att Mr. Hodgkinsons. I treated Cous Johnson, D. [? R.] Langton, and Mr. Franks, att Turlagh's. An unhappy accident fell out between M [? N—Nabby] and me.

Ye 6th.—Frost continues. Nabby was very ill all last night, by means of ye late accident. All is well again. We had newes that Tirconnell had resign'd and fled into France, and that most of the considerable places in ye Kingdome had declar'd for ye P of O. A stranger preach'd this afternoon.

Ye 7th.—Frost continues. R. Piggott, Johnson, and I walk't to Penwortham, where we mett severall gentlemen, and walk't to Boat house, and came home wth Coll.

Ye 8th.—Some haile and sleet which froze as it fell. I was wth Mr. Mayor, who is in great perplexity about the choosing men to goe to Convention. He this day receiv'd the circular letter. Ld Derby recomends his brother.

> The men to whom reference is made were the two who had to be elected M.P.'s for Preston.—Convention means the Convention Parliament about to be summoned. A circular letter was sent out by the Prince of Orange to the various boroughs, ordering the burgesses thereof to return members to the Convention Parliament, which was to meet on January 22nd, at Westminster, and the communication referred to was a letter of this kind.— Lord Derby was William George Richard Stanley, the 9th Earl, and the brother recommended by him was the Hon. James Stanley.

Ye 9th.—A thaw. In ye evening I was wth ye Rigbye Capt and his brother, and others, att Rigby's, very merry.

Ye 10th.—A great thaw. I saw Walton copp overflowen. I was wth ye mayor and Coll. All night Nabby was ill, but proves a false alarm. I rode out wth cousen Johnson. Patten and Rigby make great interest for election. Mr. Stanly is sure to be one.

> Walton cop—an artificially raised bank, running along a portion of the south-west side of the Ribble, between the present police station and the houses at the north end of Walton village, near the bridge, and intended to protect the adjoining road, land, &c., from flood water.

Ye 11th.—A fresh frost. Ill newes from Ireland. I was wth one of Bellfast, att Rattliffs. I gott some Guinnyes. Monsieur Bryan gott a soare hurt on his nose. I visited him, etc.

Ye 12th.—Frost in ye morning ; thaw'd in ye afternoon. This is call'd ye great Saturday, but a very slender markett ; no goods goe off. I was att Rigby's wth Capt W. Clifton and his brother James and one Mr. Westby, all R, who seeme very high upon ye newes of Tirconnell houlding out.

> Great Saturday was the name given to an annual horse fair at Preston— it was called Great Saturday Horse Fair. For a very long while it lasted a whole week—the first week after the first Sunday in the New Year; in January, 1879, the time of it was reduced to three days; in 1905 it was limited to two days; and as thus curtailed so it remains.—The two Cliftons were William and James (brothers of Sir Thomas Clifton) ; Mr. Westby would be a member of or connected with the Westby family, of Mowbreck Hall, near Kirkham ; and they were evidently all Roman Catholics—" all R."

Ye 13th.—A frost and thaw. About 2 this morning Naby [Nabby] fell into labour, and so continu'd in much paine till past nine att night, att wch time she was deliver'd of a lusty daughter.

Ye 14th.—A frost and thaw. I was wth ye mayor and above 18 more of ye best of the town, and payd beverage for my daughter. Rigby and Patten will not stand to theyr agreement about election. I was desir'd to personate ye E of Derby's brother.

Ye 15.—A frost and thaw. This day was ye election of members to serve in the Convention [Parliament]. Mr. Stanly, whom I personated, was unanimously chosen. Ye competition between Rigby and Patten was carried by 2 votes for Patten : he had 208, 'tother 206. I was carry'd on mens shoulders from barrs to barrs, and was handsomely treated till very late.

> Mr. Stanley was the Hon. James Stanley. He was a Whig. Only in one Parliament did he sit as a member for Preston. He was M.P. for Lancashire from 1690 to 1702, when, through the death of his brother, he

succeeded to the peerage as the 10th Earl of Derby.—Rigby was most likely Edward Rigby—grandson of Edward Rigby, Serjeant-at-law, who was one of the members for Preston from 1661 to 1681.—Patten was Thomas, a Whig, the eldest surviving son of Alderman William Patten; the latter being a son of Thomas Patten, of Patten, near Warrington, who was an ancestor of Colonel Wilson Patten (afterwards Lord Winmarleigh).—The "barrs" were the toll bars in Preston, at the time in question three in number, viz., one in Fishergate, near the top of Mount-street, another in Church-street, near the end of Water-street (now Manchester-road), and the third in Friargate, between Edward-street and Bridge-street (the latter now merged in Marsh-lane). Many years ago these bars were done away with.

Ye 16th.—A great thaw, but without much raine. I was to take leave of Mr. Patten in order to his journy to London. I sent 7 Guineas by him. I was wth W. Patten, Capt. Pigot, and others, and came home in good time.

W. Patten was a son of Alderman William Patten, and the diarist's cousin.—Capt. Pigott may have been Mr. Robert Pigott (or a relative of his) referred to in the note to the entry for Oct. 9th, 1688.

Ye 17th.—A thaw. This afternoon abigail was baptised in the Church. Cousen W. Patten godfather, and Cousens Johnson and Betty Bickerton godmothers. I had ye mayor and some of ye best of ye town. I was att night wth Capt Longworth and some other Justices who kept sessions here this day and receiv'd certificates of all dputy Lewts and magistrates of this side of ye country.

Abigail was the diarist's daughter (named after his wife), born on the 13th of this month. She survived till 1770, unmarried, and was buried at Castle Bellingham.—Capt. Longworth would be Richard Longworth, gent., of Larbrick, near Poulton-le-Fylde.—The Justices were county ones, obviously, and the sessions they attended would most likely be of the special kind.

Ye 18th.—A great mist. I receiv'd severall letters from Ireland, but all speak of great preparations there, and yt T [Tirconnell] will not surrender. I saw Richmond from lerpoole [Liverpool], who confirms ye [report of] men being drown'd in Dublin Bay, and

[that] Coll Sarsfeild was among them. I was wth severall others att cards, at alderman Sudalls, till 'twas late.

> Sarsfield was not amongst the men said to have been drowned. He accompanied James II to Ireland in the following March, when he was made a Privy Councillor and a Colonel of horse. Next he became a Brigadier. He was at the battle of the Boyne as Major-General, and he escorted James in his flight to Dublin. After considerable service on the Jacobite side, in Ireland, he went to France; and in 1693 he was mortally wounded at the battle of Landen.

Ye 19th.—A fayr day. I was wth Mr. Fleetwood and his cousen Dick who sayes he heard by a vessell come from Ireland last Sunday yt ye Protestants there were in good posture of defence. I was after wth severall women att ye coffee house, and so att Mittons, and came home very late, etc.

Ye 20th.—A misty day. Mr. Franks came from Liverpoole, and brought an account yt ye Protestants in Ireland were in a good posture to defend themselves. I was wth Mr. Chaddock and others at Mittons.

Ye 21th.—A misty day. Cousen Johnson and R. Piggott and I went to see Bramhalls fine horse. He asks £100 for him : he is a comely, large horse, chesnutt collour'd, but has no gate. We cross'd ye foord by lower path. 'Tis a pleasant situation, and much orcharding about it. There are 20 acres inclos'd wth a stone wall. From thence we came to Cuerdale, Mr. Ashton's, and din'd there, where I saw ye largest child of 3 years and a halfe old. He is 3 foot and a half tall and near an inch. We came to Preston about 2 a clock. We were treat'd with canns [of wine or ale] by R. Piggott, this being his birth day. Att night we play'd att cards at Dr Lees. Sr John Coghill was for some time in this town to-day, and seem'd very desirous to see me. He has brought his family out of Ireland, and plac'd them att Lancaster : himselfe is gone for some time to London ; so I was disappointed.

> R. Piggott was Robert Pigot. He was a son of George Pigot, of Preston, gent., and was the Mayor's Bailiff at Preston in 1684-5.—Bramhall must have been a person on a visit or but temporarily sojourning in this locality : there was no regular resident of Preston at this time named Bramhall.—The "foord" (ford) referred to would be near Brockholes old mill (disused for a long time), where passage across the Ribble was obtained by means of stepping stones.—For a great number of years members of the Assheton or Ashton family successively owned and occupied Cuerdale Hall, on the south bank of the Ribble, and about a third of a mile below the ford referred to. When the diarist visited the Hall it was, presumably, the residence of William Assheton, by whom it was partially rebuilt in 1700. The previous owner and occupier (Richard Assheton) married a sister of Robert Pigot before mentioned. Cuerdale Hall is now a farmhouse. In the neighbourhood of the Hall—on the west side and near the Ribble—there was unearthed, in 1840, a lead chest, in which were found numerous ingots and ornaments of silver, and also about 7,000 coins (English, French, &c.) bearing dates ranging from A.D. 814 to 900, supposed to have been hidden at a time of national trouble or when some serious conflict was feared.—Sir John Coghill was Master in Chancery in Ireland. He was the seventh in descent from John Cockhill, of Cockhill, who was in the reigns of Richard II and Henry IV living at Knaresborough.

Ye 22th.—A fayr day. I had letters from Ireland, and ye Sligoe declaration. Att night James Charlton came hither, who had been att Gernonstoune a weeke agoe. He gives a dismall account of Ireland, especially of our county, from whence most of ye Protestants are fled. We saw ye German shew his tricks. I saw Sr J. Coghills sonne.

> Our county was Louth.—The tricks of the German were most likely of the conjuring kind.

Ye 23th.—A misty, moyst day. Mr. Chaddock had newes of ye arrivall of his vessell at Liverpoole from Burdeaux. I was att night wth the master, one Lucas, who sayes that ye french inveighed mightily against ye English and Dutch. He confirm'd ye account of ye french seizing a dutch ship att Plymouth and murdering all ye men. Mr. [H]arrington of Kendall was here, who gave me an account of his knowing Sr J. Coghill.

Ye 24th.—A moyst day.   Here came soldiers and officers from Carlisle, going to Warrington, from whence they expect to be sent into Ireland ; yt there was one Tranbar Etheridge and one Cornwall whose parents are in Ireland.   I had ye German to shew [his tricks] before my wife and some other gentlewomen att my lodgings.   I was wth ye officers att ye mitre and Mittons.

Ye 25th.—A moyst day.   Ye soldiers march't out early.   Post came in late.   Ye Lords and Commons address'd ye P of O wth thanks and desir'd his continuance of ye Regency.   I was att night wth Hodgkinson, Chaddock, Hornby, and others at ye Dogg, and after att cousen Patten's.

Ye 26th.—A fayr day.   Nabby sweat.   I saw young Clayton, who sayes that severall passengers came to Liverpoole from Ireland, that Tirconnell had taken severall protestant soldiers who were deserting, and bound and imprison'd them, yt ye Protestants there are in great consternation and endeavouring all they can to escape for England or ye North, yt Tir. threatens if any forces land from here he will turn his army loose to doe what they please.

Ye 27th.—A fayr day.   I walk't wth Mr. Croston to Walton, where we heard one Coulton preach and read prayers very well.   I was wth Dr Lee and others att Rattliffe's.

Mr. Croston was the Rev. Richard Croston, headmaster of Preston Grammar School.—Coulton was a stranger or non-resident.

Ye 28th.—A wett day.   I tooke Physick which wrought very well.   Dr Lee and severall freindes came to visitt me.   This afternoon came in some men who are design'd for Ireland—in ye meane time to quarter here.   They are very promising men.

These men would be soldiers.

Ye 29th.—A moyst day. Little newes but what is bad from Ireland. Att night I was wth Mr Richmond, Chaddock, Mr Mayor, and others att Rattcliffe's, etc.

> Mr. Richmond would be Dr. Richmond previously referred to, or a relative of his.

Ye 30th.—A fayr day. Having no prayers this morning, ye Collonell, Mr. Croston, and I walked to Walton. From thence a a large Circuite, by Cann bridge. I sup't and din'd. About 5 a clock Mr. Langton came and sate with us till 10.

> Cann or Can Bridge is in what is now called Higher Walton, a thriving little place about a mile e.s.e. of Walton-le-Dale village. At the time of the diarist's walk there would be very few, if indeed any, houses here. The bridge crosses the river Darwen.

Ye 31th.—A moyst day. I went with ye Coll and his Lady to Penwortham. From thence Coll and I went to Hutton and grange, and somewhere ye water had made a great breach on a curious marsh. We din'd att Penwortham, and came home early. R. Piggott and Mr. Syl Richmond have had a quarrell.

> The Colonel (Rawstorne) and the diarist would no doubt go to Hutton Hall, owned by the former, and a comparatively new building at the time, having been erected in the earlier part of the same (17th) century. It is at present the residence of Lawrence Rawstorne, Esq., a descendant of the Colonel.—Grange was Hutton old Grange, about two miles west of the Hall, and near Hutton Marsh at the side of the river Ribble.

Feb. ye 1st.

A fayr day. We had ye account of ye house voting ye K. to have abdicated ye Realm, and ye throne thereby become vacant. Ye Commons had only 8 dissenting votes. In ye Lords' house 48 were for governing by Regency and 51 for no Regent. I tooke a decoction and electuary of Dr. Lee's. I was late wth Dr. Roe, etc.

> On January 28th the Commons, as "a Committee of the whole House," resolved without a division that the conduct of King James II had been unconstitutional, &c., and that having gone out of the kingdom he had abdicated the Government, in consequence of which the throne had become

vacant. Next day the Lords decided by a majority of 51 to 49 against a
Regency. Two days afterwards the Lords debated amongst other things
whether the throne was vacant, and resolved by 55 to 41 that it was not.

Ye 2d.—A fayr day. We had prayers, but very maimed. Robert
Rigby was buried this afternoone, and Gregory preach'd his funerall
sermon. I was wth Mr. Fleetwood and others, first att Ratcliffes
and then att Tirlaghs, etc.

Ye 3d.—A fayr day. Some clashing in ye Convention. One
Bland, a probationer for ye Curacy here, preach'd in ye afternoone.
I saw an officer treat a souldier very severely. We walk'd on
Enam, and tooke 3 canns in ye Weend. A sore toe.

> The place where the diarist took—supped—the cans of drink would
> probably be Main Sprit Weind.

Ye 4th.—A moyst morning. I was wth Dr Roe and some of
ye officers att ale. My toe pains me very much. I rec'd a noate
to be assisting to a freind, which I answear'd, and compos'd ye
difference

Ye 5th.—A fayr day. Dr Lee, Mr Langton, and I went to
Poulton. We call'd att Bradkirk, and stay'd about an hour wth
Mr. Parker, and were receivd very kindly by Mr. Hornby. Mr.
Harrison, ye Vicar, and Mr. Heardson came to us.

> Mr. Parker would be either Christopher Parker or his son Anthony.
> The Parkers resided at Bradkirk Hall, near Kirkham, and were, it is said,
> "relatives and dependants of the Derby family."—Mr. Harrison was
> probably one of the Harrisons, of Bankfield, within Singleton Grange, near
> Poulton-le-Fylde.—Mr. Hornby would be Edmund, of Poulton-le-Fylde,
> gent., or Richard, of Greenhalgh-with-Thistleton, near Kirkham.—The
> Vicar was the Rev. Richard Clegg, of Kirkham Parish Church.—Mr.
> Heardson may have been Augustin Heirdson, of Poulton-le-Fylde, or a
> relative of his.

Ye 6th.—A fayr day. Capt Veal came to us. We went a
coursing, and had an excellent course. Capt. Westby, Mr. Parker,
and young Westby mett us, and came and din'd wth us. In ye

evening we went to see Mr. Barton's mother and sisters : one is marry'd to one Peatson, and ye other, Mrs (i.e. Miss) Prudence, is unmarry'd ; she is pretty but inclinable to grow fatt.

> Capt. Veal was the son of John Veale, of Whinney Heys, in Bispham, the nearest town to which place, at the time of the diarist, being Poulton-le-Fylde. Whinney Heys was situated on a hill: " the present farm house is only an abridgement of the ancient hall." (Tyldesley Diary, note p. 170.)—Capt. Westby was a member of the Westby family of Mowbreck Hall, near Kirkham—probably John, who married Jane, daughter of Christopher Parker, of Bradkirk Hall.—Young Westby would be a brother of the Captain.—Mr. Barton was, according to Fleetwood's diary, " an Irish preacher," and a " Fellow of Dublin College."—Peatson was James Patteson, of Poulton-le-Fylde.

Ye 7th.—A fayr day. Mr. Hornby went early to Liverpoole. We came away [? from Poulton-le-Fylde] about 11 o'clock. Overtook Mrs Parker in her Rollioon wth 2 sisters. I call'd att Freckleton. Saw Mr. Sharpless wife of Dublin. Came to Mr. Chaddocks ship, att ye nebb of Neas. Met Mr. Richmond there. Eat and dranke and play'd about an houre. Got home before 5 of ye clock. Saw Mr. Kennyon att Mr. Hodgkinsons, and play'd a game att Tables wth him.

> In none of the dictionaries—general or provincial, old or new—is Rollioon met with. It may be a word meaning a small, low-set vehicle, having for its prefix, Rolley—a word signifying a diminutive underground waggon without sides; or it may refer to a thick, rough cloth dress termed a Rullion or Rallion.—The call at Freckleton, on the way from Poulton-le-Fylde to Preston, would necessitate a divergence of a few miles southward from the ordinary road.—The nebb of Neas (Neb of the Naze) is a small and somewhat elevated projection at the side of the river Ribble, about a mile south of Freckleton village.—The ship referred to would be moored in or at the mouth of Freckleton Pool, just above the Neb of the Naze.

Ye 8th.—A fayr day. I was wth Mr. Kennyon all ye afternoon. Ye Lords and Commons can not yett agree about ye words abdicated and deserted. I was late at play att Mr. Hodgkinson's, and lost some money to Mr. Kennyon.

> The words mentioned refer to James II. See Macaulay's History, Cap. X.

Ye 9th.—Some raine last night : a fayr day. I sent my dogg to be taught. Nabby was Church'd. I gave my sisters bill to Marsden's man. Was wth Mr. Hornby and Sharpless, and after wth Mr. Fleetwood.

> Sharpless would be a person from Dublin—evidently the husband of the woman alluded to in the entry for the 7th of this month.

Ye 10th.—A dry day. We had ye account of ye P and P of O [Prince and Princess of Orange] being declar'd K and Q [King and Queen] by ye Lords. Ye curate preach'd a very ingenious sermon about unity. I saw Mr. James Ashton, who came lately from Ireland.

> On February 6th, after a free conference between the Lords and the Commons, the former decided by 62 to 47 that James II had abdicated the Government, and then the same body resolved, without a division, that the Prince and Princess of Orange should be declared King and Queen.—The curate who preached would be the Stipendiary Curate of Preston Parish Church.—Mr. James Ashton was elected an Alderman of the Preston Council in 1672; he was twice Mayor of the borough—in 1674-5 and 1683-4; and on the 13th of September, 1687, the Council relieved him of his Aldermanship "because of his absence from the town and necessary frequent residence in Ireland."

Ye 11th.—A dry day. We went a coursing towards Lea ; kill'd a lease of hares ; din'd att Swansy's ; came home in good time wth ye officers, and went after to ye Serjeant's. This day was ye drunken jury. Nabby went home to her nurse.

> A lease or leash of hares is a brace and a half.—Swansey's would be near the west corner of Preston Marsh.—The Serjeant's, i.e., the house of one of the municipal Serjeants—probably that of the Mayor's Serjeant.—Respecting "Ye Drunken jury," they may have been a mock, perambulating, bibulous set, having some connection with Shrovetide conviviality.

Ye 12th.—A windy day. Great cock fighting. Sr Tho Stanley lost every battle. I had good newes from Ireland, yt ye Prot[estants] were in good posture of defence. I was a little while wth Mr. Fleetwood and others att ye bowling green house, and came home early.

There was a public cock-pit in Preston considerably anterior to 1650. At the time of the diarist there was cock-fighting, which he patronised, at a place on or near the west corner of Preston Marsh. Some of the Stanleys had a keen penchant for this class of sport. Edward, 12th Earl of Derby, caused a cockpit to be made near the west end of Preston Parish Church—about 30 yards from it; in this pit many of his game birds fought; and it was kept open for fighting purposes till 1830.

Ye 13th.—Some raine. Cocking continues. Coll St. John's came to this town. He confin'd Lewt. Roche. I was wth him, and treated him att ye Dogg, and after sup't wth him att ye anchor where I stay'd late and dranke.

Ye 14th.—A fayr day. This being appoint'd a thanksgiving for our deliverance from popery, etc., we had prayers and a sermon. After dinner I was wth ye mayor and officers att Coopers, and then I treat'd ye officers att a bowl of punch att ye anchor and stay'd late. Capt Collier came this day to town.

Ye 15th.—A moyst day; much rain in ye night. Coll. St. Johns went home. We had an account of ye Pes of O [Princess of Orange] landing att London on Tuesday last. One Mr. Peper of Ireland and his wife came to this town. Here came Dean Pullein, Mr. Mead and Lee, 2 Bulleris, Ellwood, and Billy Graves. They landed att Whithaven, and bring a most dismall account of affayres in ye north. I wrote a very long letter to my cousen Frowde, to be communicated to my Ld Clarendon, about ye present state of affayres there. Stayd wth ye Dean till very late.

The Princess was very cordially received; but her apparent levity of manner, on reaching Whitehall, tended to militate against what should have been unqualified appreciation. Singular to say, not until after her death was a vindication of her conduct issued: this was done by the Duchess of Marlborough, who averred that the peculiar demeanour mentioned was in reality due to a spirit of thorough disinterestedness and self-devotion, and

not to any carelessness or impropriety of feeling.—Dean Pullein was the
rector of St. Peter's, Drogheda.   Later he became the Bishop of Dromore.—
The persons whose names directly follow that of the Dean were from Ireland
—presumably from the north of the country.—Cousin Frowde married Sarah,
daughter of Sir D. Bellingham, and widow of George Blount.

Ye 16th.—A fayr day.   Dean Pullein and ye gentlemen came
to pay my wife a visitt, and so went to Liverpoole.   Capt Wescomb,
son to ye late Consull att Cadiz, came to town.   I was wth him att
ye mitre, and after Capt Stoughton treat'd ye Mayor, Aldermen,
Mr. Fleetwood, and severall others, att ye Serjeant's, where we were
entertain'd wth wine, anchioves [anchovies], and excellent musick.

> Capt. Wescomb's father was Sir Martin Wescombe, Bart.—Capt.
> Stoughton seems to have been sent to Preston for some military examining
> or supervisional purpose, and it is very probable he came from Liverpool or
> Chester.

Ye 17th.—A moyst day.   We had an acct of ye new King and
Queen being proclaim'd last Wednesday, att London, wth much
joy.   Capt. Wescomb went hence.   Mr. Franks payd away [? his
way] att Rigby's, being to goe for London.

Ye 18th.—A dry, cold day.   This morning came a letter from
ye King and Counsell, directed to ye Sherriffe or to ye
Coroners, to Proclame the new K and Q [King and Queen], wch
was done wth great solemnity att ye Cross.   After we went to ye
mayors, so to Mittons, then to ye bonfire, and from thence to
Tirlaghs, att all wch places we drank theyr healths; ye soldiers
fir'd severall volleys; and concluded all wth bonfires and ringing
of bells.

> The proclamation would be made at Preston by the Mayor.   The
> Coronership of the borough and its precincts was, with other offices,
> conferred upon the Mayor here by the charter of Queen Elizabeth, granted
> in 1566.   The last charter, granted in 1828 by George IV, not only confirmed
> this but made the immediate ex-Mayor and the senior Alderman borough
> coroners.—This plan of coroner-making was afterwards abolished.   The
> Municipal Reform Act, which came into force at the end of 1835, empowered

SIR JAMES BELLINGHAM, Bart.,

Who built and restored the greater part of Levens Hall.
(From a painting in the collection at Castle Bellingham).

the Council of every English and Welsh borough which had a separate court of quarter sessions to appoint a fit person, not being an alderman or councillor, to be coroner of the borough. The power of appointing coroners is now vested in County Councils.—The Cross was the principal one in the town : it stood in the centre of the Market Place.—The bells which were rung were those at the Parish Church.

Ye 19th.—A hard frost. Nabby was very ill. Ye curate, Mr. Bland, is return'd. I tooke Lodgings att Mr. Walmesleys for my sister. I fell out wth my friend. Att night I was wth Mr. Pepper, of Ireland, and Mr. Walmesley. One Woodwood [? Woodward] att Mr. Mayors, a lame clerke, spoake very saucily to D. Langton, and sayd yt ye rising on ye Blundering Saturday was to cutt ye Papists' throats. Cousen Peers.

Mr. Bland, previously mentioned as a " probationer " (see entry for the 3rd of this month), would now be the stipendiary curate at Preston Parish Church.—The diarist's sister was Mrs. Ann Bickerton.—Hezekiah Woodward, feltmaker, of the city of Dublin, who was an in-burgess of Preston and apparently a native of the town, had two sons (Samuel and Timothy), and the clerk may have been one of them.—Cousin Peers was an Irish cousin, on Sir Daniel's side.

Ye 20th.—A wett day. Nabby continues very ill of a looseness. I din'd att my cousen Patten's, where we entertain'd ye Ladyes wth ye musick.

Ye 21th.—A wett day. Nabby recovers. We din'd att my cousen Patten's, and sup't att cousen Johnson's, and had a bowl of Punch. Ye women, all but Nabby, were very peevish and ill humour'd.

Ye 22th.—A fayr day. We were going parte of ye way wth cousen Peers and Betty gott a violent fall, of which she was dangerously ill. I receiv'd letters from Ireland yt ye Prot[estants] were 40,000 strong. I dranke wth T. Banks, and went late home wth cousen Peers. Ye men muster'd.

Ye 23th.—A fayr day. I receiv'd my sister's mony. Betty B recovers. Some papists disarm'd, but theyr swords restor'd them again. Capt Stoughton and Rock came and play'd with me att Grand Trick track. I was [afterwards] wth Mr Fleetwood and others att Turlagh's.

> Rock was Lieutenant Roche, mentioned in the entry for the 13th of this month.—Grand trick track was a game similar to back-gammon.

Ye 24th.—A fayr day. Mr Gregory preach'd in ye morning and the Curate in ye afternoon. I din'd wth Capt Stoughton att cousen Johnson's. Betty recovers well.

Ye 25th.—A fayr day. Stoughton, Coll, etc. We went to Penwortham: cours'd and din'd there. Went to ye town, and where some words happen'd between Roch and little Heron, and a lye was given. We part'd them, and came home early. Ye gout troublesme.

> Heron was not a local person. Probably he was, like Roche, of the military order.

Ye 26th.—A very fayr day. Mr. Gregson went towards London. I went as far as Whittles wth him. Came home by Lealand, where I saw Capt Wescomb and Mr. Wamsly. Sr J. Coghill was again here to see me. I receiv'd ye declaration for Ireland. I am very ill wth my toe, and Nabby has taken a violent scowring wch much indisposes her. Capt Stoughton receiv'd an express to give a faythful account upon word and honour w[hat] effective men there are in these companyes. I play'd wth him att grand trick track att Coll. Rawstornes.

> Whittles—Rose Whittles being the full name—is a hamlet a mile east of Leyland village, about six miles from Preston, and on the main road "towards London." The companies would be quartered or would muster at Preston.

Ye 27th.—A very fayr day. Nabby was dangerously ill last night, but tooke some powders and Julep, and is much better.

I gott a stray'd horse which was challeng'd and taken from Yorkshire.

Ye 28th.—A stormy, wett day. I went wth cousens Patten and Johnson to Goosnar. Mr. Threlfall and his wife came and din'd wth us and brought a brace of carps. We were very hearty. I saw Capt Stoughton after I came home. My cousen Patten was ill. Nabby recovers. I feed Dr. Lee this morning.

> Mr. Threlfall was either Cuthbert Threlfall, of Ashes, in Goosnargh, near Preston, who died in the autumn of 1692, or one of his three sons—perhaps Edmund, a very keen Jacobite, whom the diarist may have visited in order to sound him, and who was killed, whilst making resistance after having been surprised, by some militiamen, near Ashes, in the summer of 1690.—" I feed Dr. Lee," &c., means paid him for professional services.

March ye 1st.

A dry day. We had a report of K Ja [King James] landing in Ireland. Betty fell very ill of fitts. I was wth Capt Wescomb and his Lady att night.

Ye 2d.—A fayr day. Betty recovers and tooke Physick. I was wth Capt Wescomb and his Lady, and treated them att ye mitre, and after went wth ye mayor and Mr. Fleetwood and others to Margarett Mittons, and stayd late and dranke too much.

> Margaret Mitton was a landlady, either the wife or widow of an innkeeper previously mentioned (p. 30).

Ye 3d.—A fayr day. Mr. Bland preach'd a sharp sermon against ye Papists. Mr. Gregory preach'd in ye afternoone against anger and revenge. Sarah Clifton was bury'd.

> Sarah Clifton was the daughter of Widow Clifton before named (p 40).

Ye 4th.—Some raine. I was in company wth Mr. Withers, Captain of ye Grenadiers. I chang'd for severall Guineas. Dean Pullein came to this town from Liverpoole. He was att Chester and Rixam [? Wrexham]. He brings a sad account from Ireland yt

Mr. Downs and severall of ye Colledge came from thence last Friday. Christ's and St. Pattricks Churches and ye round Church are made into garrisons. Tirconnell has disarm'd all Protestants att Dublin, ransack'd ye colledge for armes, sends 20,000 men speedily into ye North, and dayly expects ye late King.

> Captain Withers was not a local gentleman, he was probably from Liverpool or Chester. The round church, since rebuilt, is the present St. Andrew's Protestant Episcopalian Church, Dublin.

Ye 5th.—A fayr day. Dr Pullein went hence for Lancaster. I went to dine att Penwortham wth ye Captaines, and, hear[ing] yt a vessell arriv'd att Stanner end wch came from Ireland and brought newes of ye Dutch being landed there, I posted away thither, but found it a lye. I came backe and found ym [them] att ye Boat house, where I stay'd for some time, and came home in the darke.

> Stanner End, now called Stanner Point, is a projecting piece of land, on the north side of the river Ribble, between Freckleton Pool and Warton sands.

Ye 6th.—A fayr day. Mr. Newcomen and Lanty Dowdall were here. I din'd with them, and after dinner was most of ye afternoon till 12 att night wth Coll. St. Johns. Some little words happen'd from D. Langton, wch he heartily asked Pardon for. I went home wth ye Mayor. Nabby and Betty tooke Physick this day.

Ye 7th.—A fayr day. Coll St Johns went hence. Mrs. Fleetwood came to town and payd us a visitt.

Ye 8th.—A fayr day. I walk'd this morning. Little newes. I was with ye officers att shooting, and after came to Ned Cravens, where we had stinking oysters ; so to ye mitre, to punch, where Coll and I left them.

Ye 9th.—A fayr day. I din'd att ye anchor wth ye officers. Went and shott wth them att butts and after play'd at tables.

> The shooting butts were on Spital Moss, on the north-west side of Preston.

Ye 10th.—A fayr day.   Mr Croston preach'd a learned sermon on ye doctrine of meritt, and Mr Bland [preached] in ye afternoon.

Ye 11th.—A fayr day.   Lewt Webster came to town, and brought newes of ye late K[ing] being taken, but it gains no creditt.   I sup't wth ye officers att ye mitre.

Ye 12th.— A fayr day.   I saw Capt Withers exercise his company of Grenadeers.   Coll. Rawstorne receiv'd severall lers [letters] of ye Papists Caballing.

Ye 13th.—A fayr day.   Johnny Shepheard came here and brings a most prodigall account of Ireland.   He gave me money to keep, and I treated him and ye officers att ye Dogg, where we stayd late.

Ye 14th.—Some snow this morning.   I went to Garstang and mett wth Sr J Coghill, Dr Pullein, Capt Longworth, Mr. Robinson, etc.   We were very merry.   Parted about 5, and gott home in very good time.

Ye 15th.—A dry frost.   Ye fayr proclaim'd.   I was wth ye Mayor and officers, and after treated J. Shepheard att ye anchor.

Ye 16th.—Much snow and very dirty.   I was wth Capt Bury, who is quartered at Crossan.   My cousen Patten payd his way.

> Crossan must be intended for Croston, in the hundred of Leyland, about eight miles south-west of Preston.   The hamlet of Crossens, on the south-west coast of the Ribble estuary, would be a place far too much out of the way for any military quartering purpose.—Payd his way, i.e., treated the company he was in on the eve of a journey.

Ye 17th.—Rain in ye morning.   Mr. Walmsley, of Lealand, preached 2 excellent sermons on Contentment.   I was with an ensigne, Price, and ye officers att ye Mitre, and sup't att my cousen Pattens.

> Mr. Walmsley was the Rev. George Walmesley, Vicar of Leyland from February, 1684-5 till his death in the latter part of 1689.

Ye 18th.—A fayr day. My cousens Patten went hence for London. I went wth them as far as Whittalls. J. Shepheard went to Liverpoole. I was att night wth Mr. Atherton, minister, of Liverpoole.

> Whittals means Rose Whittles—a hamlet near Leyland village, already referred to.—Mr. Atherton would be the Rev. William Atherton, who became Rector (mediety) of Liverpool, along with the Rev. Robert Styth, in 1699, when Liverpool was detached from Walton-on-the-Hill and made a separate parish. He continued joint Rector till his death in 1706.

Ye 19th.—Much raine. We heard of ye revolt of Dumbarton's regiment att Ipswich. Capt Bubb, of Carlisle, was here, wth whom I dranke att ye mitre. 7 Irishmen were sent hither, by Sr Richd Standish, suspected to designe for the North to meete Oglethorp.

> Oglethorp was Sir Theophilus Oglethorpe, Brigadier-General of James's army. After the flight of James, Oglethorpe was deprived of his military emoluments; then he went to France; and subsequently he took the oath of allegiance to King William III.

Ye 20th.—A very wett day. I went to ye house of Correction, and spoke to Nicholas Collier, one of ye Irish men, who confess'd yt he heard yt K Ja [King James] was in Scotland, that Newcastle had declar'd for him, and yt ye Lancashire men would rise to his assistance. I saw Tho Whitehead, lately escap'd from Ireland. He goes to Kirkham. I saw Mr. Greenfeild.

> The House of Correction at Preston was on the west side of the town. It occupied a portion of the site, if it did not actually absorb a very considerable portion of the structure, of the old Friary—a building which, after the Dissolution, was occupied for a time as a private residence, and subsequently, probably about 1680, transformed into a gaol called the House of Correction. It was supplanted as a prison, in 1798, by the present gaol on the east side of the town. (Preston Court Leet Records, p. 65).—Thomas Whitehead was presumably a son of Benjamin Whitehead, of Preston, gent., and may have been related to some of the Whiteheads who were living in or about Kirkham at this time.

Ye 21th.—Very much raine. We had an account that there was a great engagement in Ireland, that the Protestants lost 4,000 and the Papists 6,000 men, but yt ye Prots kept ye field ; but ye master of ye vessell affirms that he saw severall officers brought into Drogheda desperately wounded. Capt Longworth wrote a letter to Coll Rawstorne intimating ye great feares the country was in of the Papists who were very insolent. Ye Captaine came to town. I was wth him.

Ye 22th.—A very fayr day. I saw Dean Ward, who sayes ye newes of an engagement in Ireland is wholy false, that Sr William Franklin is in Liverpoole and brings an account that all the Northern forces were joyn'd and resolv'd to maintaine their ground. The copp att Walton has a a great breach made att one end of it. I rode out in ye afternoon to view it. I secur'd three Irish soldiers.

> Dean Ward was the Rev. Thomas Ward, B.D. In 1679 he was made Dean of Connor, co. Antrim. He was likewise Vicar General. In 1694 a Royal Commission deprived him of the Deanery.

Ye 23th.—Much raine. Mr Peatson and Mr Hornby were here from Poulton[-le-Fylde.] They gave me an account of Mr. Barton being there. We have endeavour'd to engage him to be here [at Preston] to administer the Sacrament att Easter. Sr John Mullineaux came here. Ye officers return'd from Wiggan.

> Mr. Peatson would be James Patteson of Poulton.—Mr. Barton was the "Irish preacher," &c., before referred to.—Sir John Molyneux was the third baronet of Teversall, Nottinghamshire—a branch of the family of Molyneux Earls of Sefton. He married Lucy, daughter of Colonel Alexander Rigby, of Middleton, in Goosnargh, near Preston, and at or about the time when the diarist was at Preston he owned some property in the town. (Preston Court Leet Records, p. 130).—The officers referred to were military ones.

Ye 24th.—A fayr day. Mr. Bland preach'd twice very well. We have a certaine account of K Ja [King James] being landed in Ireland and the deserters laying down theyr armes. I walk'd wth ye officers att evening to see Walton Copp, which is so much damag'd by the flood that it is thought £400 will not repayr it.

March 25th, 1689.

Some snow and sleet in ye morning. I walk'd to Enam Garden.
Capt Wescomb and his wife came to town. I was with them att ye
mitre. A soldier was buyred. Severall of them are very ill wth
drinking. Nabby walk't to Walton Copp, but came home very
weary.

> The new year commenced on the 25th of March and this plan was
> observed until 1753, when, through an Act of Parliament passed in 1751
> (24 Geo. II), a change took place. By the statute referred to it was enacted
> that the 1st day of January, 1753, should be the first day of the new year,
> and so in all subsequent years.

Ye 26th.—Snow and raine. I receiv'd ye dismall account from
Lancaster of ye Protestants' defeat in ye North of Ireland, and that
severall made theyr escapes to England, Scotland, and Londonderry.
This Dr Lee brought wth a letter from Dean Pullein.

Ye 27th.—Much snow. We had severall of ye defeated of ye
North come to this town. They confirme ye newes and that the
Irish are now in possession of all but Londonderry. I walk't wth
R. Piggott and D. Langton to Walton.

Ye 28th.—Much snow in the morning; afternoon very fayr. I
walk't a great while wth Capt Withers at Enam.

Ye 29th. Much raine. One Gillibrand preach'd. Mr. Barton
administred ye Sacrament. I was wth him in the afternoon.
Alderman Sudell's child was bury'd.

> Gillibrand may have been Jonathan, son of the Rev. Jonathan Gillibrand,
> who was enrolled a burgess of Preston at the Guild of 1622, was Vicar of
> Leigh, in Lancashire, for 23 years—till his death in 1685—and was the son
> of the Rev. William Gillibrand, Rector of Warrington, from 1607 to 1620.

Ye 30th.—Very much raine last night and this morning. Mrs.
Threlfall brought me a brace of large carps. I invited Mr. Barton
and Mr Bland to dinner. After dinner I was wth Mr. Fleetwood,

who receiv'd a letter that there was a person seiz'd att Whitehaven wth letters to ye Convention of Scotland and to some papists of this county.

Ye 31st.—A wett day. The Sacrament was administred. I received. Mr. Barton gave it, and preach'd 2 incomparable sermons. Sr Henry Ponsonby came hither from London. He gives a dismall account of his escape. I was wth him and others att the anchor.

> Sir Henry Ponsonby, Knt., of Bessborough, co. Kilkenny, married a daughter of Capt. Shaw, of Drogheda, in 1674, and died in the reign of William III, when the family estates passed to his brother, William Ponsonby, who in 1721 became the first Viscount Duncannon.

Aprill ye 1st.—A very wett day. Sr H. Ponsonby went very early. I had an account of ye sad defeat in ye N of Ireland, and yt honest Will Ponsonby was kill'd. I was wth ye Mayor and Mr. Barton and others, and after we were late att Mr. Hodgkinson's.

> Will Ponsonby may have been related to Sir Henry; but, if the account as to his having been killed were correct, he could not have been Sir Henry's brother mentioned in the preceding note.

Ye 2d.—A very wett day. Great shooting att butts. Ye Yorkshire man lost. Here came an order for ye companyes to march to Liverpoole and Ormskirke. Tomlinson, Bolton, and Whitehead came hither. We were up late.

Ye 3d.—A fayr day, only some few showers. Ye companys march'd away, and return'd againe by a counter order. Dean Pullein and Alderman Singleton came hither. I sup't wth them att ye anchor and stayd till it was very late.

Ye 4th.—A very fayr day. Sr John Coghill came here. I treated my friends att my Lodgings. Dined wth them att ye anchor. They went away after dinner. Barton, Whitehead, and I diverted ourselves att play, and att night I was wth Capt Davis, sonne to

Hercules, who is going to Berwicke. Capt Stoughton came from Liverpoole. He saw ye forces embarque, who went off wth very great alacrity.

Ye 6th.—A fayr day ; some raine in ye evening. Here came 3 troops of Collonell Langton's regiment, who suppress'd the mutineers of Ipswich. I payd my way to ye mayor and severall others.

> The mutineers consisted of a Scotch regiment. They objected to go on Continental service, to help the States General against France ; but they were not suppressed at Ipswich. They went north, by forced marches, eventually being obliged to surrender near Sleaford, in Lincolnshire, to a body of horse soldiers, under the command of Ginkell, a very able Dutch officer, brought over by William. Later, this same Scotch regiment was much engaged in Continental campaigns, and distinguished itself very excellently.

Between this and ye 6th of May I was att London. Ye weather generally very fayr. On ye 6th of May I return'd wth my sister and neice.

> The sister and niece were Mrs. Bickerton and her daughter Betty.

May ye 7th.—A fayr day. I bowld wth Coll St. Johns, etc. Express came from Liverpoole yt Derry holds out still.

Ye 8th.—A very hott day. I din'd wth ye officers and sate wth ye Coll till near 12 att night.

Ye 9th.—A hott day. I din'd wth Cousen Johnson, bowl'd, and was att dancing wth ye officers, att Mrs Tophams, wth some of ye young ladyes of ye town.

Ye 10th.—A hott day. Mr. Sharpless came to see me. Major Roe came to town. I saw Mr. Griffith and payd him ye 10 Guineas wch his brother sent me.

> It is not unlikely that Mr. Griffith was from Liverpool.

Ye 11th.—A hott day. Ye battalion of 7 Companyes drew out and exerciz'd well. I din'd wth ye officers. Made upp accounts with my sister and Mrs. Gregson.

> Probably Mrs. Gregson was the wife of Josiah Gregson, Town Clerk of Preston, previously mentioned (p. 14).

Ye 12th.—A hott day. Hughes, Chaplain to Kirk's Regiment, preach'd an excellent sermon. Capt Berry and I walk't to ye boat house to see Tom Fleetwood. My wife, sister, and the girls came to us. Birch preach'd in the afternoon.

> The person whose regiment is referred to was Colonel Percy Kirke, whom Macaulay, in his History of England, describes as " a military adventurer, whose vices had been developed by the worst of all schools, Tangier."— Capt. Berry was presumably Wm. Berry, of Ormskirk, gent.—Tom Fleetwood was connected with the Fleetwood family of Penwortham.—Birch was the Rev. Thomas Birch, Vicar of Preston Parish Church.

Ye 13th.—A fayr day. Ye Battalion drew out. An express came for them to march immediately to Ormskirke. I went parte of ye way wth them, and was wth Capt Withers, Develin, and Bickerstaffe late.

Ye 14th.—A hott day. Ye King's declaration of Warr against ye French King. I sup't att cousen Patten's and eat chard.

> Chard is a variety of white beet, producing large juicy leaves, and having a solid rib along the middle. The chard of artichokes has a tender central leaf-stalk blanched.

Ye 15th.—A very hott day. I walk't in ye morning. Went to ye Marsh in ye afternoon, and saw Mr Parker, etc.

Ye 16th.—A fayr day. I play'd att Mr. Chaddocks, and was treated. I walk'd wth Nabby on Enam.

Ye 17th.—A windy day. Mr Kenyon came to town. 5 justices of peace sworn. I was wth Mr Kenyon and them.

Ye 18th.—A fayr day and wind for ye forces who are gone to
Derry. Some hail in ye evening. I was wth Mr. Fleetwood and
his cousen, of banke, late.

> Mr. Fleetwood's cousin would be Christopher Banastre, of Bank Hall, in
> the township of Bretherton, about nine miles s.w. of Preston. For centuries
> Bank Hall was the manorial residence of the Banastres or Banisters
> (Baines's History of Lancashire). Many Banastres were for a long time
> connected with Preston.

Ye 19th.—Some raine in ye night. Ye Curate preach'd in ye
morning and Mr Gregory in ye afternoon. I walk'd to Walton and
saw Mr Houghton.

Ye 20th.—A rany morning wth some hail. Ye wind N.W.

Ye 21th.—A fayr day. I din'd wth ye Mayor att Penwortham.
Mr. Barton and French came to this town. I was wth them late att
ye anchor.

> Formerly there were burgesses of Preston named French. They came to
> the town, from co. Bedford, in the early part of the 17th century, and seem
> to have ceased residing in it some time between 1660 and 1670. The
> person of this name mentioned by the diarist may have been one of them, or
> a descendant.

Ye 22th.—A fayr day. Shooting at bootts [butts] between
Fletcher and Etherington. Fletcher won. After went to the
marsh and bowl'd. Stay'd late with Mr. French.

Ye 23th.—Much raine this morning. Mr. French went hence.
Serjeant Walls was buryed. We supt att W. Patten's.

> Serjeant Walls was Anthony Wall, gent., who was elected Town's Serjeant
> in October, 1688.

Ye 24th.—A fayr, temperate day. Sr John Coghill gave me an
account of another great defeat given by those of Derry to ye

beseigers.   I was with Char. Rigby and Mr. Gibbs.   I receiv'd a
letter in great haste from Sr J. Coghill yt his sonne lay very ill.

Mr. Gibbs was the Rev. Thomas Gipps, Rector of Bury, who qualified as
an out-burgess of Preston at the Guild in 1682, on which occasion he was one
of the special preachers in connection with the festival.   He was Rector of
Bury from 1674 to the time of his death in 1712.

Ye 25th.—Some raine.   I was wth Sr Rich Standish and Mr.
Fleetwood.   There came in a detachment of Dragoons of Collnel
Leviston's.   They are 60 besides officers.

Ye 26th.—A fair day.   This morning about 4 I fell very ill,
tooke a vomitt, and began to mend about 10.   Mr Gibbs [Gipps]
preach'd twice.   I had several visitants, among them Mr. Gibbs.

Ye 27th.—A fayr day.   I bowl'd in ye afternoon wth ye Lewt.
Coll. Matthewes, and sup't att cousen Patten's.

Ye 28th.—A fayr day.   I saw ye Dragoons exercise very well.
Great cocking att ye marsh.   Some Dragoons went out this evening
to search for Papists' armes.   I tooke ye bitter draught this
morning ; wrought well.

Ye 29th.—A fayr morning, but a very wett afternoon.   I was att
ye marsh, and saw severall matches att cock fighting.

Ye 30th.—A fayr day.   I went wth ye officers to ye marsh, and
bowld most of ye afternoon.   Ye Dragoons return'd wth severall
Papists' horses, but little worth.

Ye 31st.—Much raine ; ye wind att S.   We hear that Kirke is
again off.   I bowld wth ye officers, and went to see cousen Patten,
newly come from Lancaster.

June ye 1st.

A fayr day.   Mr Hornby came to see me.   I bowl'd in ye afternoon, and walk't wth Nabby.   Dick Awdes dy'd this morning about 2.

> Mr. Hornby would be Edmund Hornby, of Poulton-le-Fylde, gent.—Dick Awdes may have been Richard Awrds, of Poulton-le-Fylde, or a son of his.

Ye 2d.—A fayr day.   Coll Matthewes and me walk't in the evening.   He treated us att his quarters.   Dick Awdes was buryed this afternoon.

Ye 3d.—A very wett day.   Coll Matthewes was wth me att my Lodging.   Mr. Franks came home.   Margaret fell ill.

Ye 4th.—A fayr day.   I went with Mr. Rishton to Poolton [Poulton-le-Fylde].   I had soar eyes.

Ye 5th.—A fayr day.   We went to Martin Mear to fish.   We heard great guns from Lerpoole.   Din'd att Capt Veales.

> Martin Mear, i.e., Marton Mere, is in the old parish of Poulton-le-Fylde, and about two and a half miles south-east of Blackpool.   Centuries before the diarist's time it attracted fishers.   In the reign of Edward III there was litigation as to the right of fishing in Marton Mere (Baines's History of Lancashire).   Anciently this Mere was six miles long and at least a mile and a half wide.   On old Lancashire maps it is very clearly defined as Marton Mere and Marton Moss (Fishwick's History of Poulton-le-Fylde).   In 1854-55 much land in the district was drained, in accordance with a plan devised and carried out under the supervision of the late Mr. James Fair, of Lytham, and this tended to considerably diminish the quantity of water in the Mere.   Since then, through additional drainage and the accumulation of sediment, there has been a further reduction of it; but the aqueous area is still about 20 acres.   The Mere contains a great deal of fish—principally pike —and is very considerably frequented by water fowls.—It is hardly likely that guns fired at Liverpool would be heard at Marton Mere, the distance, in a perfectly straight line, being 31 miles.   Probably the guns were discharged somewhere in the neighbourhood of Formby Point—a nearer place, also more open, and thus giving greater freedom for reverberation.

Ye 6th.—A wett afternoon.   I came from Poolton.   Called att Mr Parkers [Bradkirk Hall], and gott home about [no time mentioned] of ye clock.

Ye 7th.—A fayr day. I bowl'd both fore and afternoon wth Coll Matthewes. Was att Kellett's att night.

Ye 8th.—A fayr day. I bowld wth ye officers and treated them att Cook's. Mrs. Ashton was buryed.

> Mrs. Ashton would be the wife of one of the Ashtons, of Cuerdale Hall, on the east side of Preston.

Ye 9th.—A fayr day. Nabby was very ill of a cold and stayd from church. I had an invitation from Mr. Gipps for Mr. Barton to be chaplain to ye E. of Derby.

> Mr. Gipps—the Rev. T. Gipps—owed his position as Rector of Bury to the "E of Derby" (the 9th Earl) mentioned by the diarist. He was presented to it by the Earl.

Ye 10th.—A fayr day. There came some letters to Coll Matthewes from Cockermouth. I was wth Mr. Walmsley, of Lealand.

Ye 11th.—A fayr day. Mr. Tim Bankes was here, going to London. Mr. Barton came and sup't with me. I gott answer from Drs Comons [Doctor's Commons] serv'd.

> Mr. Tim Banks, whose name has already appeared (pp. 3, 15, 53), was, it is well nigh certain, Timothy Banks, a lawyer, who figures in Bellingham documents of this date.

Ye 12th.—A hott day. I went wth Mr. Barton, Hodgkinson, Patten, to Bury, by Bolton. Stayd all night wth Mr. Gipps.

Ye 13th.—A hott day. Went to Manchester by Prestwich. Call'd on Mr. Ashton ye Parson. Saw my Lady Stevens and her daughters. Att Manchester is a very good Church. It is a rural Deanary, wth very bad Choristers. There is a good foundation of

Hospital boys, founded by one Chetam of this town, and a pretty Library wth an annual income of £10 p an.

> Mr. Ashton was the Rev. William Assheton, B.D., Rector of Prestwich. He was instituted to the Rectory here in 1685, and held it (along with the Rectory of Carlton-in-Lindrick, near Worksop, to which he was preferred in 1682) till his death in 1731.—Lady Stevens was probably connected with the Stevens family of Great Torrington. Members of this family have resided there since the time of Charles I.—The very good Church was the Manchester Collegiate or Old Church, which was constituted a Cathedral in 1847.—The Hospital and Library alluded to were founded by the bequests of Humphrey Chetham, merchant and manufacturer, of Clayton Hall, near Manchester, and Turton Tower, near Bolton. By his will, dated December 16th, 1651, he bequeathed £7,000 for Hospital purposes—for maintaining, clothing, educating, bringing up, &c., " forty healthy boys, born in wedlock, the sons of poor but industrious parents." He also devised £500 for housing the boys, the governor, officers, &c. And he left about £3,000 for a public library, which now contains upwards of 40,000 volumes. Both the Hospital and the Library bear his name.

Ye 14th.—A fayr day. We din'd wth Mr. Ashton [Rev. W. Assheton] att Prestwich. Dr Roe went wth us. We were very handsomely entertain'd. We sup't wth Dr Roe. I saw Alderman Percivall, and Mr. Hawekes, J. Banks, Mr. Tige, and Mr. Clements, all of Ireland.

> Dr. Roe was Dr. Richard Wroe—" Silver-tongued Wroe "—who was warden of Manchester Collegiate Church from 1684 to 1718. His family possessed property at Unsworth, in the parish of Prestwich, for three or four generations. He was the son of a yeoman (Richard Wroe), of Heaton Gate, in the same parish. One of the Wroe family (Jane, daughter of Robert Wroe, of Heaton Gate) was the mother of Humphrey Chetham, founder of the Hospital and Library previously referred to. Dr. Wroe was a notable preacher: he had a fine presence, possessed a melodious voice, and was styled " Silver-tongued Wroe." He was presented to the vicarage of Garstang (Churchtown) in 1684, and held it for twelve years, when he resigned the position. In 1695 he became Rural Dean of Manchester. He died on the 1st of January, 1717-18, and his remains were interred in a vault under the choir of Manchester Collegiate Church. (Palatine Note Book).—Some of the gentlemen mentioned were not " of Ireland," i.e., residents or natives of that country, but were from Ireland, where, no doubt, they had been temporarily sojourning.

Ye 15th.—A fayr day. About 11 we left Manchester. Stay'd some time att Chorley. Met Alderman Sandyford, who gave us an

account of a Papists ship that came from Ireland to Lancaster, that
severall Papers and Commissions were seizd—come from K James
to severall persons of this country, but directed to women. Here
came ye Ld Brandon, Gerard, and Capt Kirby, in order to rayse ye
militia of ye whole county.

> Alderman Sandyford was from either Manchester or Liverpool—
> presumably from the former—and had, perhaps, been at Lancaster (at this
> time a comparatively brisk shipping place) on business.

Ye 16th.—A fayr day ; wind at E, but turn'd in ye afternoon.
Ye curate preach'd an ingenious, honest sermon for unity.

Ye 17th.—A fayr day. Ye militia come in apace. Severall
Papists seiz'd. I was to see Andrew Moore, of Drogheda.

Ye 18th.—A moyst day. Ye militia drew out to ye moore. I
went to view them. I was after to waite on Sr Rich Standish, but
was disappointed.

> The Moor was on the north side of Preston.

Ye 19th.—A fayr day. Ye militia drew out. I was att ye
moore. Ye Ld Brandon and others went to meete ye Lds Comrs
[Lord Commissioners] to Lancaster. This being ye fast, there was
preaching, but no occasional prayers.

> The fast would be for the success of the fleet, &c., of William III.

Ye 20th.—A fayr day. Mr. Bankes came to see me. We
walk't out to view ye Militia. The Lds Comrs came to town very
late. We have ye certaine account of Edinburgh Castle being
surrounded.

Ye 21th.—A moyst morning. Ye Mayor treated ye Lds
Comrs. They went away about noone. Att Night I was wth
Coll Kirby and his uncle and some others.

> Colonel Kirby would be either Roger of Kirkby, near Liverpool, or a
> gentleman bearing the same name of Peel, near Lytham—probably the
> former.

Ye 22th.—A fayr day. I waited on ye Ld Delamere, who was
very obleiging. Mr. Bankes went hence. I sent my Ld Derby's
and Mrs Gipps letters by Mr. Sharpless to Mr. Barton. I was
wth Sr R. Standish, and Mr Fleetwood, and others, pretty late.

> Mrs. Gipps would be the wife of the Rev. T. Gipps already alluded to.

Ye 23th.—A very hott day. We had newes that Richards could
not gett into Derry, the river being block'd upp by a boome. I
saw blacke George Mr [? Mac] Cartney of Belfast.

> The seige of Derry was now going on. The boom was fixed across the
> Foyle, on the north-east side of the city.—George Macartney, a Captain of
> Horse, M.P. for Belfast, attainted by King James's Parliament at Dublin,
> 1689; ancestor of the Ellison-Macartneys and Earl Macartney who died
> SP. 1806.

Ye 24th.—A very hott day. Dr Leigh and I din'd att Penwortham. We had duck hunting in ye afternoon, and call'd att ye
boat house.

> The duck hunting would be on or near the Ribble, at the north side of
> Penwortham.

Ye 25th.— A hott day. We hear yt Kirke is gott into Derry.
One Skrostamore, a Dutch Quarter-master Generall, return'd hither
from Whithaven where [he] has been to secure shipping and
necessaryes for transporting men for Ireland. Severall expresses
passed to and from this town this day.

Ye 26th.—A hott day. I bowl'd att ye marsh. Severall papists
were brought in here by Sr Wm. Pennington.

> This was Sir William Pennington, the first baronet, of Muncaster, son and
> heir of Joseph Pennington, of Muncaster, who married Margaret, daughter
> of John Fleetwood, of Penwortham.

Ye 27th.—A hott day ; but some few drops of heat. There
was great shooting between Brown and Fletcher wth Billington and
Etherington. Ye former won. Att boat house att night. There

was dancing att Mr. Greenfeilds: Coll Matthews and Coll Rigby's daughters and some others.

> Drops of heat, or heat drops, are large drops of rain which occasionally fall, somewhat wide apart, when the weather is close and sultry.—Greenfeilds was the house of Christopher Greenfield, attorney-at-law, in Preston. Subsequent to this he was for some years one of the M.P.'s for Preston, and in the course of his membership he was knighted.

Ye 28th.—Some gentle showers. I bowl'd, and after went to Mr Cottam's garden to eat fruite etc.

Ye 29th.—A fayr day. Dr Roe came hither I was wth him while he stay'd, and att evening wth Mr. Mayor and Mr. Hornby att ye mitre.

Ye 30th.—Much raine. I stayd from church in ye afternoon to write Letters. Ye militia are to goe—some to Wiggan, some to Manchester, and some to lancaster

July ye 1st.

A hott day. Nabby and I went to Liverpoole. We baited att Rufford, where Mr. Barton came to us. Mr. Gregson and Mr. Rishton and theyr wives accompanyd us so farr.

Ye 2d.—A fayr day. My brother and sister Giffard came to us. We saw severall freindes. I bowld att ye green.

> Elizabeth Handcock, sister of the diarist's wife, married Duke Giffard of Castle Jordan.

Ye 3d.—A fayr day. I bowld. Dr Richmond and severall others were wth me, att my Lodging till it was late.

Ye 4th.—A fayr day. Capt Matthewes treated us att ye Lyon. I bowld, and some of us dranke ale att ye Cookes.

> The Lyon would be an inn.

Ye 5th.—A fayr day. We parted wth our freindes, and came home about 7. There went an express to Lerpoole [Liverpool].

Ye 6th.—A fayr day. Mr Barton came here. I went out to see a battalion of ye Ld Castleton's regiment exercise. I was wth Mr Barton and others pretty late.

Ye 7th.—A fayr day. Mr. Barton preach'd in ye afternoon. I went and sate some time wth Dean Ward.

Ye 8th.—A close, hott day. The Corporation rode ye boundaryes. We were handsomely treated at Capt Claytons, and was wth Mr Hodgkinson and Mr. Barton.

> Periodically the Mayor, Corporation, &c., of Preston, went along the boundaries of the borough for the purpose of viewing and confirming their course and stopping encroachments thereon. The custom was usually called " boundary riding ": some who participated in it rode on horses, but the bulk walked; and it was kept up till about 1835 (Preston Court Leet Records, p. 66, note).

Ye 9th.—A very hott day. Mr. Barton and I were treated att Mr. Hodgkinson's, and were late att ye anchor wth Coll Fairfax and other officers of Lord Castleton's regiment.

Ye 10th.—A hott day. Mr. Hodgkinson, Mr. Barton, and I went to Ormskirke to meete Mr. Roper. Din'd there and went to waite on Coll Fairfax att our returne.

Ye 11th.—A close, hott day. Ye Earl of Devonshire's regiment of horse came here. They are indifferently well mounted. Mr. Barton went to Poulton [Poulton-le-Fylde]. I bathed.

Ye 12th.—A hott day. A battalion of Sr George St. Georges regiment came hither. I saw cornett Meredith and Capt. Cursett, and recommended Tim Bankes to ye Capt.

> Sir George St. George, Bart., was a grandson of Sir George St. George of Carrickdrumrusk, co. Leitrim, and was raised to the peerage of Ireland, as Lord St. George, in 1715.

Ye 13th.—A very hott day. Ye remainder of St. George's regiment came in. I saw Ja: Barry and was late wth him.

Ja. Barry was a military captain.

Ye 14th.—Much raine. Mr. Walmsly, of Lealand, preach'd 2 apologetick sermons on unity. I walk't wth Capt Barry att Enam [Avenham], where we found ye soldiers robbing ye garden. We came after to ye Dogg, where were Capt Taylor and severall other officers.

Ye 15th.—A fayr day. I din'd att Penwortham, and went wth Mr. Fleetwood's and Coll Rawstorne to ye town end.

Ye 16th.—A fayr day. Sr Henry Ingoldsby's regiment came hither. I was to waite on him and Capt Coote who has his Lady and children wth him. I saw young Disney who wth Harry Moore are both ensignes.

Ye 17th.—A fayr day. I walk't wth ye Coll to ye marsh and bowl'd, and was late wth severall officers att ye anchor.

Ye 18th.—Much raine. This morning Nabby had an issue made. Ye soldiers unslated the Popish Chappell. I was to visit Tracy who killed Malone att Wiggan. I was wth Sr Henry [Ingoldsby] to waite on Mrs. Coote, and after wth Capt Purefoy and others.

The chapel mentioned was the first post-Reformation Roman Catholic place of worship opened at Preston. It was situated in a sort of court, which afterwards became known as, and is still called, Old Chapel Yard, on the west side of Friargate, and it was opened in 1605. At that time it was a little thatched building. It was used as a Catholic place of worship till 1761, when it was supplanted by a new chapel a short distance southward (Hewitson's History of Preston). Prior to being used as a chapel, it is very probable the little building referred to had been occupied as a cottage.— Capt. Purefoy was of the Warwickshire family, seated at Caldecote.

Ye 19th.—Some raine. I sent Mr. Bankes horse to Liverpoole. I saw Tom Whitehead and Ensign Harry Moore.

Ye 20th.—A fayr day. I saw Mr Kennyon and was wth Collnell Kirby and Rawstorn att widdow Cliftons, and were treated by Mr. Brockalls.

> Mr. Brockalls would be John Brockholes, of Claughton Hall, near Garstang.

Ye 21.—Some drops of heat. Mr. Palmer, Chaplaine to this Regiment, preach'd in ye morning. This evening came here Capt Ed. Griffiths, in his journey to Whithaven.

> At this time Whitehaven seems to have been a pretty busily engaged port in connection with transit to and from the North of Ireland.

Ye 22.—A fayr day. Ye Regiment exercis'd att ye marsh and fir'd bulletts. I din'd wth Capt Griffith att ye hind. We walk'd after noon, and sate late upp att night.

> Ye hind means the name of a local eating-house or inn.

Ye 23.—Much raine last night. Capt Griffith went hence this morning for Whithaven, and several officers went to Chester for money. I bowld in ye afternoon. We had a good account from Capt Billings of ye state of ye Protestants of Derry and Eniskillin.

> Chester was at this time the headquarters of the military forces of William III on the north-west coast.

Ye 24th.—A fayre day. The regiment went hence for Wiggan. I din'd att ye marsh. Councellour Kearnes came through with an express from Kirke to Schomberg. Derry holds out bravely, and it is hoped that Kirke will relieve it.

> The Duke of Schomberg was the principal general of William III.—Colonel Kirke was in charge of an expedition which had been despatched from Liverpool for the relief of Londonderry, and which arrived in Lough Foyle on the 15th of June.

SIR DANIEL BELLINGHAM, Bart.,

Uncle of the Writer of the Diary, and First Lord Mayor of Dublin.
(From a portrait in the collection at the Mansion House, Dublin).

Ye 25th.—A very fayr day. Ye regiment return'd. A woman of them allmost kill'd another in the Carte with a Grenadeers hatchett. I was wth Sr Harry [Ingoldsby] and we bowld, and Coll Kirby, Rawstorne, and I dranke a bottle wth him at Clifton's.

Ye 26th.—A fayr day. I play'd wth Hamilton att Trick Track.

Ye 27th.—A fayr day. Ye Regiment went hence to Wiggan.

Ye 28th.—A fayr day. Mr. Gregory preach't in ye afternoone. I sent coppyes of Capt Withers letters to London.

Ye 29th.—A fayr day. Mr. Barton and Bankes came here. I was wth Mr. Kennyon. Din'd wth Coll Matthews, and payd my way att Coopers.

Ye 30th.—A fayr day. I went by Liverpoole to Chester to view ye camp. I was kindly treated att Mrs Holt's

Ye 31th.—A fayr day. I saw ye camp. There were 8 Regiments. Schomberg came to view them. I din'd in Capt. Purefoy's tent, and sup't wth ye Lord Drogheda, where was Ld Lisbourn, Coll Wharton, Sr Hen Bellass [Bellasis], and severall others. We dranke hard and talk'd high. Here came in this day 2 French regiments. A man ran ye Gantlope. 10.

"To run the gauntlet" was formerly a not uncommon expression, and it is still occasionally heard; but the word gauntlet in such phrase is wrong. The word used by the diarist—gantlope—is, phonetically, the correct one, Phillips, in his World of Words, says that to "run the gauntlope is a punishment among soldiers, the offender having to run with his back naked through the whole regiment, and to receive a lash from a switch from every soldier. It (the word gauntlope) is derived from Gant (Ghent) a town of Flanders, where the punishment was invented, and the Dutch word lope, running."

August ye 1st.

Some raine. 5 Regiments march'd out to Nesson. I was very
ill after last night's debouch.

> Nesson must be intended for Neston, a town in Cheshire, on the south-west
> side of the peninsula formed by the estuaries of the Mersey and the Dee, and
> opposite Flintshire.

Ye 2d.—Much raine. 6 Regiments march'd out. I was wth
Sr Josuah allen. A French Regiment came and march'd out wth
ye camp. I march'd by ye camp att Nesson [Neston], and came to
that att Highlake [Hoylake] where Schomberg was. I saw a great
fleet. Here came in a man of warr from our London fleet, which
she left off Hollyhead, and the Bonaventure from Kirke which
gives an account that 2 provision ships were pass'd Culmore, going
into Derry, and yt they retooke ye Ormond Dogger and another
small vessell att ye Isle of Mull. Sam Green and I came late over
ye ferry att Lennen, where were Ld Lisbrn and Wharton They
would not lett our horses come in theyr ferry [boat]. We came in
a small cock boate.

> Sir Joshua Allen was a merchant, of Dublin; Lord Mayor 1673; father of the
> first Viscount Allen.—Highlake, i.e., Hoylake, is on the Cheshire coast, Dee
> side, about 10 miles north-west of Neston.—For some time before 1318 there
> was a ferry across the Mersey from Birkenhead to Liverpool. The right to
> work it and appropriate its proceeds was vested in the Prior and Convent of
> Birkenhead by letters patent from Edward II. This ferry crossed the river
> from Birkenhead Priory, and it used to be called "Monks' Ferry." From
> Eastham to Liverpool there was a ferry, the right to work which belonged to
> the Abbey of St. Werburgh. At or about the same time there were other
> ferries across the Mersey farther up its course. In none of the old local
> maps or histories that I have been able to meet with is there any mention
> made of the place (Lennen) where the diarist crossed the Mersey; but, as
> Highlake (Hoylake) was the last place he appears to have halted at, prior to
> proceeding to the ferry, the presumption is that he would cross the river by
> the nearest or most convenient way, and that would be by Monks' Ferry (not
> in existence now), which was between two passages across the Mersey, long
> afterwards established, and known as Woodside and Birkenhead Ferries.—
> A dogger is a two-masted fishing vessel, something like a ketch, and
> specially used by the Dutch. In the 17th and 18th centuries doggers were

often utilised for privateering purposes.   The Ormond Dogger mentioned by the diarist may have originally belonged to the Duke of Ormonde.—Ld Lisbrn was Lord Lisburne—the Ld Lisbourn mentioned in the entry for the 31st of July—and probably the John Vaughan who became the first Viscount Lisburne and who died in 1721.—Wharton was no doubt the Coll Wharton referred to in the same entry.   On the death of his father he became Lord Wharton.   He was a gay, audacious, clever man ; at one time owned the best stud in England ; was passionately fond of outrunning horses which belonged to Tory gentlemen ; was the author of that odd and at one time astonishingly attractive ballad called " Lillibullero " ; posed as a great duelist, was a keen politician, &c.

Ye 3d.—Much raine this morning.   Mr Green and I came to Preston, and called at Rufford.

They would call at Rufford Hall, the seat of the Hesketh family.

Ye 4th.—A fayr day.   Mr Coulton, of Walton, preach'd here twice.   I sup't wth Mr. Green att Mr. Mayor's.

The preaching would be at Preston Parish Church.

Ye 5th.—A fayr day.   I din'd at Mr. Lemans [Lemon's].   We saw a rail att Penwortham marsh.   Bowld att Swansy's, and dranke wth ye mayor and cousen Green att Rigby's.

A rail, i.e., a bird—a water rail.—The Greens were cousins, living in Dublin.

Ye 6th.—A fayr day.   Mr. Bankes went hence to Kendall.   I walk'd to Penwortham to visitt Mr. Fleetwood, who is very ill.   I was att night wth Mr. Preston, of Hooker, Cousen Bellingham, and others.   My sister is removed to Mrs. Bushells.

Mr. Preston was from Holker Hall, in the parish of Cartmel.   " Holker Hall was the family mansion of the Prestons, as early as the reign of Queen Elizabeth, from whom it passed by marriage to the Lowthers, and from them to the Cavendish family, the Duke of Devonshire being the present owner " (Baines's History of Lancashire).—Mrs. Bushell was probably the widow of one of the sons of the Rev. Seth Bushell, D.D., who was Vicar of Preston from 1663 to 1682, or she may have been an unmarried daughter of that rev. gentleman, for when the entry was made in the diary Mrs. was a contraction, meaning Miss as well as Mistress.

Ye 7th.—A fayr day. I bowl'd att ye marsh. We receiv'd joyfull newes of Derry's being reliev'd and ye seige raysed. It came by Capt Withers in ye Dartmouth. Here are great rejoycing by bells ringing, bonefires, and we dranke a bowl of punch att cousen Pattens.

> The siege lasted 105 days, being raised on the night of the 31st July. The Dartmouth assisted the Mountjoy and the Phœnix to break the boom.

Ye 8th.—Much raine. Captain Griffith came to town wth a squadron of Coll Coy's Regiment. We visited Mrs Pullein and Mrs. Singleton. I din'd wth ye Mayor, and sate att night wth Capt Griffith.

> Mrs. Pullein would be the wife of Dean Pullein of Drogheda, &c., and Mrs. Singleton was, presumably, either Margaret Singleton, of Haighton, near Preston, who died in or about 1697, or Jane Singleton (widow of Brian) of the same township, who died in 1707.

Ye 9th.—A fayr day. I bowld wth ye officers. Ye other squadron came to town. I was late wth Capt Griffith att ye mitre.

Ye 10th.—A fayr day. Ye Regiment march'd hence. After dinner I was wth Capt Nash. Cousen Bellingham and I rode some parte of ye way wth cousens Johnson, and call'd att Penwortham. In our return we found that Mr. Rigby and Nash had a quarrell wth some of ye Dragoons who came in this day. Mr. Higgison was very ill hurt.

> Mr. Higgison does not appear to have been a resident of the town. Probably he was in some way connected with the military element.

Ye 11th.—A hott day. Mr. Birch preach'd in ye morning and Mr. Clayton in ye afternoon. We din'd att Mr. Suddalls [Sudall's].

> Mr. Clayton may have been related, directly or indirectly, to the Clayton family of Fulwood, near Preston.

Ye 12th.—A very hott day. I went as [far as] Rufford wth cousen Green, where we met Capt Tho. Griffith, and din'd there. We bowld att Banke Green. This morning Counnt Solmes went off from Highlake [Hoylake] wth 13 Regiments of foote and a prosperous gale. God be theyr good speed.

> Count Solmes was an experienced officer. He occupied Whitehall, by means of Dutch troops, in 1688, for William, and did excellent service with similar soldiers in Ireland.

Ye 13th.—Some raine. Ye fayr was proclaim'd, and we were treated by bailiffe Bostock in ye town Hall.

> Richard Bostock was the town's Bailiff at Preston in 1688-89.

Ye 14th.—Much raine. Ye beast faire. Mr. Kirkby gives us an account yt our men are design'd for Carrigfergus [Carrick-fergus]. We were treated att Clifton's by my cousen Wm Bellingham.

Ye 15th.—A hott day. Ye horse fayr. J. Shepheard bought a gelding; cost 8 guinyes. I lent him 4. I att night treated cousen Bellingham and severall others, and sate upp late att widdow Cliftons.

Ye 16th.—A fayr day. Mr. Couling gives an account of Dundee's party being totally disperst. I rode out and took leave att Penwortham, and after was wth Dr Wroe att ye anchor.

> Mr. Couling would probably be either William Cowling or one of his two sons, named William and John, who if not at this time had previously been residents of Preston.—Dundee was John Graham, Earl of Dundee, who, after enjoying the protection of William for a time, northward, got the confederated clans of Scotland under his command, successfully fought William's forces, under Mackay, in the pass of Killicrankie, on July 27th, 1689, and was mortally wounded in the conflict. Afterwards the clans dispersed and returned to their homes.

Ye 17th.—A hott day. Mr. Bankes came this evening.

Ye 18th.—A hott day.   A stranger preach't.   We hear that Schomberg is gotten to Carrigfergus.

Ye 19th.—A fayr day.   We din'd wth my sister.   I treated severall att night, paying my way.

Ye 20th.—A fayr day.   Last night Governour Walker came here privately.   He was very obleiging to me.   Was nobly Receiv'd and treated att the Mayor's.   I went wth him parte of his way.   He made large professions of kindness.   Lord Cavendishe's Regiment came in.   I treated ye Mayor and others.

> Governor Walker was the Rev. George Walker.   He was a Protestant clergyman, and was the Governor, for civil purposes chiefly, of Londonderry during the siege of that city.   Some additional particulars respecting Walker will be found in a subsequent note.

Ye 21th.—Left Preston and came to Liverpoole.

Ye 22th.—Came to Chester.   Lord Delamere's Regiment came in here.   Sr John Bland confin'd [temporarily detained] some passengers wth a quaker come from Dublin.   Ye Mayor entertain'd Walker.   Sr Tho. Gore came in wth his Regiment.

> Sir John Bland was for several years M.P. for co. Lancaster.—Mr. Francis Skellern was at this time Mayor of Chester.

Ye 23th.—Gores Regiment went out.   I sup't wth Major Boyle and Cust.   Count Schomberg, Lord Maynard, came.

Ye 24th.—A man hang'd for murder.   I saw Capt Withers. Ye French Regiment came in.   Mr Bankes bought his horse.

> The French regiment was probably one of the four regiments of French refugees raised by the Marquis of Ruvigny.

Ye 25th.—The French Regiment march'd out and the Lord Devonshires Regiment came in.

Ye 26th.—I marchd out wth Lord Devonshire's Regiment to Highlake.   Could not ship, and so lay all night in ye feild.

Ye 27th.—We shipd about 8 in ye morning, in ye Scanderbegg, and saild about 3 in ye afternoon. Ye French Regiment wth us. We were in all about 33 sayle of ships. We payd severall salutes off Ormshead. We met a ship come from Derry.

Ye 28th.—Early in ye morning we made ye isle of man. We lay by for ye man of warr firing a gun. I went wth major Boyle on board some ships. About 2 in ye afternoon we made Ireland. Severall salutes pass'd among ye ships. We perceiv'd att distance a yatcht coming from Ireland.

Ye 29th.—This morning we came upp wth Copeland Isles. About 11 we met a great fleet of above 50 sayle coming from Ireland. We had an account of ye surrender of Carrigfergus 3 dayes agoe. About one we came upp wth Carrigfergus. Count Schomberg went on shoar. We anchord att night, and had a great storme. Ye wind att w and w : s : w.

> Carrickfergus, after it had been held a week for James, by two cavalry regiments, capitulated to Count Schomberg.

Ye 30th.—A great storme. We lye still on board. Some visited us, and were very merry.

Ye 31th.—We landed all our horse and encamp'd att White house. I met Capt Francis Purefoy, who carry'd me wth him to Carrigfergus and treated me very obleigingly. Sr Hen. Ingoldsby's Regiment quarter'd here. Some of them behav'd ill att ye seige. Lewis, Capt of the Grenadeeres, was dismiss'd for Cowardice.

> White House is now a village a few miles north of Belfast, and near Belfast Lough. When the landing mentioned took place, it is highly probable that the only building on the site of this village was a castle which was, presumably, of a light or white colour. This castle commanded Belfast, was the seat of the noble family of Chichester, and is said to have somewhat resembled the palace of Whitehall, in London. It disappeared—fell or was pulled down—long ago. (Macaulay's History of England.)—The siege, of course, refers to that of Carrickfergus.

Septembr ye 1st.

I view'd ye town [Carrickfergus] wch was much shatter'd wth ye Bombs, and ye walls much batter'd wth ye Cannon. Ye castle is strong and not much damaged. The army march'd to Bellfast. I waited on ye Genrll, and was kindly receiv'd by him. Disny brought intelligence from Dundalke.

Ye 2d.—We march'd from Bellfast, and encamp'd about 2 miles beyond Lisburne. Ye Generall view'd ye Camp. I lay att Mr. Redmonds, where I was very civilly treated.

Ye 3d.—Bad weather ever since our landing. This morning 2 of ye foot were hang'd for deserting. They hung in ye highway for ye view of ye army. We encamp'd beyond Drommore.

> Drommore, i.e., Dromore, is a town in co. Down, about 20 miles south of Belfast.

Ye 4th.—We marchd to Loghbrickland. Ye Generall march'd in the head of ye army. A carbine went off and shott a trooper of ye Ld Delamere's through ye hatt and kill'd a horse. Capt Brereton treated me in his tent.

> Loughbrickland is a neat little town in county Down, about ten miles north of Newry.

Ye 5th.—We came to Newry, from whence ye enemy retreated in great confusion, having ye night before barbarously burnt ye town. We encamp'd on ye North side of it, and had a most severe storme of wind and raine which blew down most of our tents.

Ye 6th.—I gott Protection from ye Duke for my tenants. There went a detachment of above 50 horse wth Count Schomberg. We march'd about 5 in ye evening. Came wthin 2 miles of

Dundalke, about 10 att night, where we stay'd all night, and sate on horse backe in the raine. There likewise march'd upp ye Earl of Meath wth some foot.

> The Duke would be Schomberg, previously Count, whom the diarist, after this entry, usually designates "ye Duke" or "ye Generall."—The tenants for whom protection was obtained would be in or about Gernonstown.

Ye 7th.—We came early this morning to Dundalke. Ye army came in entirely before 12, and encamp'd on the north side of the bridge. This town scap'd ye fury of ye enemy. We found here some stores of corne and a good cellar of sacke. I gott a quarter att Wm Gunnell's.

> A quarter, i.e., place to lodge or stay at.—Wm. Gunnell would be a resident of Dundalk, with whom the diarist had no doubt been previously acquainted.

Ye 8th.—Mr. Newbourgh preach'd. I din'd wth Coll Bury. Att evening I went out on a party wth Capt Hartop and T. Griffith to Dowdstowne, where we heard a party of ye enemyes dragoons were. M. G. [Major General] Kirke came in wth 3 Regiments.

> Dowdstown is a parish in co. Meath, near Navan.

Ye 9th.—I was introduc'd to Kirke. J. White came to town. We rode out wth ye Duke. Coll Coy went out wth a party to Louth.

> The town referred to would be Dundalk.

Ye 10th.—A party of foot and horse came wth me to Gernonstowne. Ye enemy were there yt morning and tooke Mr. Smith and Courtney. They return'd Smith after using him very ill. A deserter came in from Maxwells dragoons.

Ye 11th.—I sent ye deserter wth a letter to M. G. Kirke.

Ye 12.—Scravenmore came to Gernonstowne and drank wth me. Mr. Buttler our Curate came to us from Mr. Townlyes.

> Mr. Butler was Curate of Kilsaren, the Rector being non-resident.—Mr. Townlyes, i.e., Mr. Townley's residence, Townley Hall, near Drogheda.

Ye 13th.—We heard great shooting towards Drogheda. We seiz'd a man who was going to ye enemy ; but, having ye Generall's pass, we lett him goe on.

Ye 14th.—Capt Ed Griffith came here wth a party. We saw some of ye enemy upon the mount of Dromcath. I had severall messages that K James came wth his whole army to Ardee. We putt our small garrison in good order and kept gaurd all night.

> Drom is synonymous with Drum, and Dromcath is probably intended for Drumgath, a parish in co. Down, which would be about 15 English miles n.e. of William's camp near Dundalk, and from which camp, or some prominent point in the neighbourhood thereof, the enemy might, if on a mount in Drumgath, be seen, though perhaps but vaguely, by means of a telescope.—Ardee is a very old town, about seven miles, in a direct line s.w., from Castle Bellingham.

Ye 15th.—The alarum [alarm] continues. Ye drums are heard as from Maperstowne bridge. I sent an express to ye Generall, who brought orders for our speedy marching away, which we did, and reach'd Dundalke before one. I din'd wth ye Duke and was civilly treated.

> Maperstowne was what is now called Mapastown—a parish about two miles n.n.e. of Ardee, and it runs for two miles, the whole of its length, along the banks of the river Glyde, across which would be the bridge mentioned.

Ye 16th.—Some Eniskllin men forced some of ye enemyes troops to retreat att Maperstowne bridge. We mounted some feild peices and made entrenchments. A grenadeere was kill'd forraging. Ye enemy advanced to fane bridge.

> Fane Bridge crosses the Fane—a river which rises in cos. Monaghan and Armagh, traverses the higher part of co. Louth, and empties itself into the bay of Dundalk, about midway between Dundalk and Castle Bellingham. The bridge goes over the river towards the n.w. corner of co. Louth.

ALAN BELLINGHAM, M.P.

The last of the family who owned Levens, and went into exile with James II.
From a painting by Sir Peter Lely, in the collection at Castle Bellingham.

Ye 17th.—We view'd ye enemyes encampments. I din'd wth Kirke, and rode abroad in the afternoone.

Ye 18th.—I went wth Count Maynard to view ye enemyes camp. Our camp went out a forraging, both horse and foot. An Irish scout made a bravado and ran away. I seiz'd Tho. Percivall going to ye enemy. 2 Regiments of Eniskillin foot came in wth Coll Owsley, with whom ye Duke was very well pleas'd.

The Count was William, second Lord Maynard.

Ye 19th.—Mr Loe Green and I went to Carlingford, and were on board severall ships. I swam as I came over ye Lord Dungannon's foord. Tom Greenfeild left me. By him I wrote [? sent] severall letters.

Ye 20th.—About 3 this morning we had an alarm, but prov'd a false one. 3 troopers from ye enemy deserted and came in to us. A dragoone of ours shott one of the enemy in count Maynards view, to whom the Count gave a guinea. We have a very warm report that ye enemy intend to-morrow wth theyr whole force to attack our camp.

Ye 21th.—The enemy appeard before ye town in great numbers. They brought 12 peices of Ordnance, and made a show of attacking our trenches. We had severall light skirmishes, in all which our men shew'd great forwardness and impatience. About one a clock ye enemy drew off without making any attempt upon us. We shott 3 or 4 of theyr men. A bullett fell just by me.

Ye 22th.—Mr. Arwaker preach'd. I received ye H. Eu. [Holy Eucharist]. Visited Tom Meredith, who is very ill. Some french men deserted and more are suspected.

Ye 23th.—Ye enemy made a second appearance and burnt much forrage on this side theyr camp.   I went on board the Fan fan.

Ye 24th.—A great storme.   I payd Mr. Harbord £50, and receivd 2 bills of exchange on Mr. James Herriot, goldsmith, in fleet-street.   I wrote severall letters.

Ye 25th.—I went wth Sr Hen Ballass to Carlingford to view the hospitalls, which are all govern'd by french.   Severall French being found to be Papists are sent hither to be transported for England.   There is a great discovery of a conspiracy of severall French who resolvd to deserte.

> William's forces, under Schomberg, were encamped about a mile from Dundalk, north side, on some low-lying, marshy ground, and they suffered much from disease, which if not caused would be considerably aggravated by the position of the camp.   The hospitals would not be actually in, but near, Carlingford, a few miles from the camp.—Sr Hen Ballass (Sir Henry Bellasis) was son and heir of Sir Henry Bellasis, who predeceased his father, the first Baron Bellasis, of Worlaby; he seems to have taken the title of his father for a short time after the latter's death; on the death of his grandfather (the first Baron), in 1689—presumably quite near the end of that year—he became the second Baron Bellasis; and in 1692 he died, when the title became extinct.

Ye 26th.—Ye enemy appear'd and burnt all ye forrage near ye town.   6 French deserters were hang'd, among whom was one du Plessis, who was ye Ringleader.   2 were hang'd of Beaumont's Regiment, who were taken going to ye enemy att Charlemont. Deserters come in.

Ye 27th.—A great defeat given by ye Eniskillin men to ye Irish att Boyle.   300 kill'd and severall taken prisoners.   Here we have great rejoycing for ye victory.   Ye Cannon fir'd thrice and 3 vollyes of small shott.   2 French horsemen wounded, as is believd,

in a duell by themselves.   John Shepheard went for England in ye
Fan fan.

> Boyle is in the north of co. Roscommon.—John Shepheard was apparently
> the son of Thomas Sheapard whose name appears in the list of in-burgesses
> of Preston for 1662, and it is very probable he was related to the
> Sheppards of Broughton, near Preston, who qualified as out-burgesses of the
> borough at the Guild in 1682.

Ye 28th.—Very wett weather.   I din'd wth M. G. Kirke.
J. Shepheard went off wth a fayr wind.

Ye 29th.—Much raine.   We had newes of Bon taken by
storme.

Ye 30th.—I went wth Count Maynard wth a great party of horse
and forraging towards Bleeke's.

Oct. ye 1st.

The horse muster'd.   Ye General view'd ye enemye's camp.

Ye 2d.—Much raine.   I din'd wth Capt Pownell.

Ye 3d.—Ye Enniskillin men brought in some prisoners.   I
wrote [? sent] letters by one Nicholls and Mr. Latham.

Ye 4th.—Severall deserters came in.   Our men beat off a party
of ye enemy who beat off our sentinells.   Ye Duke off towards ye
ships.   I treated Major Kirke and Withers.

> The ships would be in Carlingford Lough.

Ye 5th.—I rode wth Comissary Sheeles to Castletown, and
went after dinner wth ye Duke towards ye enemy.   We had some
light skirmishes wth ye enemy and kill'd one of theyr horses.
Three handsome young fellowes deserted and came over to us.

> Sheeles would be Shales. "A crowd of negligent or ravenous functionaries,
> formed under Charles and James, plundered, starved, and poisoned the
> armies and fleets of William.   Of these men the most important was Henry
> Shales, who in the late reign had been Commissary General to the camp at

Hounslow. It is difficult to blame the new government for continuing to employ him, for, in his own department, his experience far surpassed that of any other Englishman. Unfortunately, in the same school in which he had acquired his experience he had learned the whole art of peculation." (Macaulay's History of England.)—Castletown is a parish two miles n.w. of Dundalk .

Ye 6th.—This morning a deserter brought word that ye enemy had burnt and quitted theyr camp. He brought off his own and his Comrades horse. Count Schomberg went out wth a party of horse and Dragoons, and was att theyr camp. After dinner ye Duke rode out and view'd the country from Dunbin Hill. I went wth Sr Hen Bellass [Bellasis] and Coll Earl and saw ye enemyes camp. They have burnt all the country near it. Kirke told ye story of ye old woman chewing ye wafer.

Dunbin Hill is in the parish of Dunbin, which is two miles s.w. of Dundalk.—The tale, it is presumable, would be one against the Roman Catholics.

Ye 7th.—Much raine last night. We had a party of Enisk [Enniskillen] men abroad, to discover ye enemy. They lye on ye 2 rivers of Gernonstown and Ardee. Joan McGuire came from home. She says there is a strong garrison there. I din'd att M. G. Kirkes. A party went towards Connoght.

The river of Gernonstown is the Glyde, and that of Ardee the Dee.—Joan McGuire was evidently in the service of the diarist at his home in Gernonstown.—Connoght of course means Connaught, directly west.

Ye 8th.—A dry day. My Ld Blany came from England. Johnson from Dublin in an open boate. Ye Danes landed in Scotland. Art went to Gernonstowne. I visited some sick freindes in ye camp. Some forces came to Carlingford, both horse, foot, and Dragoons.

Lord Blany was either the fifth lord, who died in 1689, or the sixth lord— presumably the former.—Art is perhaps a contraction, and meant for Hart as the prefix of Hartop; if so, then it will refer to Captain Hartop, previously mentioned.

Ye 9th.—Dry weather. Some deserters came in. Art return'd. I waited on ye Duke wth his account. Ned Singleton and Robin Twigg arriv'd from Garlingford [Carlingford].

Ye 10th.—A great party went out wth ye Duke. I rode a great way on ye lurgan by myselfe. Ye Fan fan came in wth Mr. Stewart. I was wth Comissary Sheeles [Shales] about my lodgings. Ye Quarter Mr [Master] Generall threatened to burne us out of our lodgings.

> On ye lurgan must mean to or towards Lurgan, or Lurgan Green.

11th.—Fayr weather. Ye horse drew out. Mr. Mason came here. I went wth him to Kirke about ye post office. I was wth Comissary Sheeles about J. White and R. Sybthorp.

> Sybthorp was of Dunany, in co. Louth, a cousin of the diarist, whose grandmother was a Sibthorpe.

Ye 12th.—Dry weather. Johnson confin'd and examin'd about the betraying Culmore forte. I went aboard a wine ship and was thrown into ye water. Mr. Holt dy'd. Mr. Mason gott his comns [commissions].

> Culmore Fort was near Lough Foyle, and about five miles n.e. of Londonderry city. This fort (conjectured to have been built in the 16th century, and much altered in the 17th) was reduced by the forces of James II at the time of the siege of Londonderry.

Ye 13th.—A stormy day. Mr. Holte was bury'd. Art went out last night and return'd late this night.

Ye 14th.—A very wett day. I went to view ye ground att Lurgan, to lay an ambuscade. Art went out.

Ye 15th.—Sad weather. Ye party suffer'd ye enemy to escape by the illness [darkness or inclemency] of the night, and had like to have shott each other. Art return'd this night, and sayes ye enemy are in a lamentable condition.

Ye 16th.—Bad weather. Ye Duke view'd all the camp and charg'd ye officers wth ye care of theyr soldiers. Sr Edw Deering dy'd last night. Toby Purcell came this day, and brings an account of ye Danes landing in Scotland, and 8000 land men putt on board our fleete, att Plymouth, for the service of Ireland.

Sir Edward Deering or Dering was M.P. for Kent, and had been a Treasury Lord. Evelyn in his diary, under date May 1st, 1680, says:— "This afternoone came to visit me Sir Edw. Deering, of Surrendon, in Kent, one of the Lords of the Treasury, with his daughter, married to my worthy friend Sir Robert Southwell, Clerk of the Council, now extraordinary envoye to the Duke of Brandenburgh and other Princes in Germanie."—The Danes would be some of the mercenaries who subsequently figured in the army of William.

Ye 17th.—A fayr day. Ye Duke rode out to ye Lurgan. A strong party came to Gernonstowne. Ye English men brought in 6 dragoons of ye enemy, 10 horses, and kill'd 4 on ye place. I din'd wth M. G. Kirke. I saw Nich Stanley, lately come from England.

Nich Stanley was not related to any of the more important people of that name—the Stanleys of Knowsley, Bickerstaffe, and Cross Hall (Lathom), in Lancashire, or those of Alderley, in Cheshire. Possibly he was connected with some of the Stanleys in the Fylde, between Garstang and Poulton.

Ye 18th.—Dreadful weather. I heard from home. Waited on the Duke, and lodged cousen Purcell wth me.

Ye 19th.—Dismall weather. Some words pass'd between Capt Purefoy and me about the lodgings. Camboon quarter'd Coll Purcell in our lodgings.

Camboon was Colonel Cambon, an officer with a superior reputation.

Ye 20th.—Continu'd raine. Mr. Newburgh made a most excellent sermon. Severall Regiments remov'd from the farr side of the water to this, theyr camp being over flow'd wth water.

The flooded camp was on the north side of the lower part or estuary of the river which passes Dundalk and flows into the adjoining bay.

Ye 21th.—The Duke sent for me. I waited on him to the Lurgan. We had a party of 150 horse and dragoons. The enemy appeard near lurgan house. I had like to have been surpriz'd by an ambuscade of 9 dragoons. Count Maynard seem'd very shy in engaging ye enemy. Art is return'd wth an account of 8 Regiments of ye enemyes decamping. I din'd wth Mr. Sheeles [Shales] and gott ye generlls pass for my servants, cattle, and goods.

Ye 22th.—Indifferent fayr. I was on board some ships to buy some beer. I gott some coales. I rode out in ye evening wth Sr Hen Bellass [Bellasis], who made great professions of freindship.

Ye 23th.—Most dismall raine. I din'd wth Lt. G. Douglass and the Count de Carelston. I rode out in ye evening wth ye Duke, and had a long conversation wth him. Most of our sick both yesterday and this are sent on board ye ships.

> Lieut.-General Douglas was Sir William Douglas, Knt., who had command of a troop of dragoons on the accession of William and Mary. He was son and heir of Sir William Douglas, Knt., of Cavers in the co. of Roxburgh, Scotland. His mother (nee Katherine Rigg, daughter of Thomas Rigg, of Athernie) was known as " The Good Lady of Cavers."

Ye 24th.—Art return'd wth an account of ye enemyes decamping and would leave 5000 in Ardee. J. White, &c., went to Drumore in ye evening. I was wth Capt Pottinger, and wrote [sent] letters by him to Nabby.

Ye 25th.—A dry day. A Court martiall held on Rich Johnson, but was left undetermin'd. Newes came of Jamestown being taken by ye enemy; 14 kill'd and 2 Lewts [lieutenants] of Dungannon being burn'd and 6 prisoners taken. I din'd wth ye Duke. A party was out att Dromiskin last night. I rode out wth ye Duke, and sate upp late att play wth some of Kirke's officers and won some money.

> Jamestown is a small town in co. Leitrim, near Carrick-on-Shannon.— Dromiskin is a parish about a mile north of Castlebellingham.

Ye 26th.—A fayr day. A man came in from Drogheda. He sayes that K James was to be there as thursday, and that great numbers of theyr men dye. I din'd wth Brigadeer Stewart, and was late wth Kirkes officers.

Ye 27th.—A very fayr day. I din'd at Major Gen Kirkes. Dean fitzGerald preach'd before ye Duke. Cornett Green was out to discover ye enemy att Tallonstowne bridge. Saw some foot dragoons and a great drove of cattle. 2 Lewts in Haumers Regiment fought Hanmore and Shepheard. Sheffield was kill'd, and lay some time unburied.

> Tallonstown is a parish in co. Louth, about nine miles s.w. of Dundalk, and the bridge mentioned crosses the river Glyde.—The fight would be in the form of a duel.—Sheffield was evidently one of the "Lewts" [lieutenants] referred to.

Ye 28th.—The Duke rode out beyond Castletown, and view'd ye severall camps. I din'd wth Mr. Sheeles [Shales]. A trumpeter came in wth ye return of some prisoners. I was late att punch wth Kirke's officers. Sr Tho Gore dy'd.

> Castletown is a parish two miles n.w. of Dundalk.

Ye 29th.—A great party of horse of near 1000 went out to discover the enemy. They went to Tallonstown, but came away without effecting anything, but took a few cattle and a sergeant, and lost a French private. Count Maynard commanded the party. I sent away my trunke, &c., towards the North. Wharton dy'd.

Ye 30th.—A fayr day. I went on board ye Phœnix. Din'd wth ye Earl of Meath and Ld. Lisburn. Was at the funerall of Gore and Wharton. This night Sr John Davis came in an open boate to Carlingford from Dublin. Art came from the North.

> The Phœnix assisted in the relief of Londonderry.—Sir John Davis would probably be an ancestor or bygone relative of Sir John Francis Davis of Hollywood, in Gloucestershire.

Ye 31th.—8 vessels came in from Carlingford.   Ye Duke sent a trumpeter (wth ye Serjeant who was taken prisoner) to the enemy. I din'd wth Major Billing.   Waited on the Duke att night, and sent out Art ; but the D [Duke] seemes to give no great vallue to any intelligence.   Green gave me an account of ye other night's adventure, att Tallonstowne, and sayes that if they had order they might have brought away some 100s [hundreds] of cattle, and could easily have fallen into ye enemyes camp.

Nov ye 1st.

I waited on M G Kirke, who was very obleiging.   I din'd wth Lord Sherborne, and att night I gott ye Duke's pass to goe for England.   2 boyes came from ye enemy wth an account of K James being returned to RD [Ardee] after having once left it, and that there is a discourse of theyr coming to attack us.

Ye 2d.—Art return'd.   There came in severall pacquetts from England.   They brought newes of a plott discover'd of 10,000 men being gone to Bristow for Ireland, and a good agreement between ye K [King] and Parliament.   Our sick are dayly sent away.

> Bristow is the recognised 17th century form of Bristol.—The King was William III.

Ye 3d.—Cold weather.   Severall of ye sick are sent in carts to Carlingford, and dye by the way.   Strict orders are given out for all soldiers to lye in theyr camp.   I was on board ye yatcht in order to procure a cabin, and came home in Sr. Jo. Topham's calash.   I saw Mr. Morris, and recieved letters from Preston.

> A calash is a light, four-wheeled carriage, low set, with a moveable top or hood, and a seat in front for the driver.

Ye 4th.—Very wett weather.   A messenger came in wth an account of ye enemyes being decamped and leaving a garrison in Ardee, which they have strongly entrenched.   In the afternoon

Joan McGuire brought me the newes of my house being burnt yesterday morning, and [in] ye evening deserting it.   Att night Franck Young came in, whom I introduc'd to ye Duke.   He sayes ye enemy are in very ill condition—they have sent most of theyr forces into winter quarters—and that K James was to goe from Ardee as to-morrow.   Lord Sherbourne and some other volunteeres are gone to Carlingford, in order to embarque for England.   Major Engoldsby and Lewt Coll Barrington are gone off from theyr Regiment, and Toby Purcell [who] met Lewt Coll Fr Young assur'd me that he saw ye Doggs in ye Irish army plucke upp theyr dead bodies and eat them, insomuch that att his coming here he was much afrayd they would fall upon him.   Here are some discontents amongst the great ones about ye mismanagement of this campaigne.   Severall of our men dyd in ye way to Carlingford, being left in ye highwaye.

> Major Engoldsby would be Sir Henry Ingoldsby.—Lieut.-Colonel Barrington may have been connected with the Barringtons who settled at Limerick, primarily in 1691, or a son of Sir Gobert Barrington, who was a Colonel in the army.

Ye 5th.—Most dismall weather of wind and raine.   I was a considerable time this morning wth Coll Stewart, who spoake freely wth me of great matters.   He seemes much dissatisfyed att ye cold reception here of the Derry and Eniskllin men, and sayes that Douglas was charg'd wth mutining, because he spoake freely about ye soldiers being abus'd for want of pay and other necessaryes. Michael, my miller, came and confirm'd ye newes of my house being burnt, and that ye tenants and neighbours were under dismall apprehensions of being all destroy'd by the Irish.

> Some of the ruins of the house are still visible, near the present castle, at Castlebellingham.

SITE OF COLONEL BELLINGHAM'S RESIDENCE, GERNONSTOWN

(near the present Castle Bellingham).

Destroyed by the soldiers of James II.   Portions of Ruins in background.

Ye 6th.—Still miserable weather. Severall officers came into our quarters, being driven by ye extremity of the weather. I sould my horse and furniture to Capt Wescomb for 18 guineas. I was late wth Kirkes officers, and was most freindly treated by them, and carry'd severall tokens from them for theyr wives and others.

> The horse would be one which had been used by the diarist in the campaign, and the furniture would be its harness.

Ye 7th.—This morning I deliver'd my horse att ye Generalls. Some horses were taken away from wthout ye lines, as was sayd by ye enemy, but beleiv'd by some of the army to the North. I sould my beavour to Rollston. I gott a certificate from ye Generall of my good service during this campaigne.

> " My beavour " would be a hat.

Ye 8th.—bitter weather—wind, raine, and haile. I came on board the yatcht Peggy Stanly, and the miller came to me from home. I received Kirkes adieu and had a noble bonefire att parting.

Ye 9th.—This morning ye Ld Hewett, Sr John Davis, Sr Hen. Ingoldsby, and severall others came on board. Our Captaine has been very active in getting the shipps to float. The Generall march'd this day from fatall Dundalke, and left behind him 3 English and three forraigne Regiments, to guard ye town till ye ships are all gott off. La Meloniere commands in chiefe.

> Ld Hewett was Sir George Hewett, Bart., who was created Viscount Hewett of Gowran on April 9th, 1689.—The many fatalities through disease at the camp, near Dundalk, account for the diarist's expression "fatall Dundalke."—The forraigne regiments were either the refugees (French), or the Danes, or some of William's Dutch troops.—La Meloniere was a colonel with a high reputation.

Ye 10th.—Severall passengers came on board.   I went on board ye Wellcome, who is left admiral here.   She is a man of war ketch. About 3 in ye afternoon we sett sayle ; ye wind at N.n.e. ; fayr weather.   Most of ye passengers very sick.   My Lord Hewets servant brought an express order from ye Duke to sayle.

> Admiral is a name applied to the ship which carries the Admiral, also to the most important or considerable vessel of a fleet.

Ye 11th.—A very fayre day.   Ye wind very changeable ; a dead calm all ye afternoon.   We were in view of Ireland, Isle of Man, and Wales most of ye day.   About six in ye evening we anchor'd wthin 5 leagues of Holyhead.

Ye 12th.—The wind came fayr at 12 att night.   We made a very fayre passage, and landed att Nesson [Neston] about 7 att night, and lay att ye key [quay] house, att George Eaton's. Sr John Davis went this night to Chester.

Ye 13th.—I went early to ye rock house.   Went over ye ferry wth Mrs. Mason.   Came to Liverpool and deliverd my lers [letters] and tokens to Kirkes officers wives.   Saw severall freinds. Left Liverpoole about 2, and came to Preston before eight, and was most kindly receiv'd by all freindes.

> An old document quoted in Ormerod and Helsby's History of Cheshire describes Rock House as " a messuage, farm, or tenement in Tranmere or Bebington."   Tranmere is a township in the parish of Bebington.

Nov ye 14th.—Some raine.   I was visited by severall freindes, and carry'd to ye alehouse, and entertain'd by them.   Mr. Birch was wth us att ye Talbott.

> Mr. Birch was the Rev. Thomas Birch, Vicar of Preston.

Ye 15th.—Some raine and sleet.   I wrote by Bradley to Ireland. poore Shepheard came ill from Liverpoole.   We supt att Cousen Patten's, and sate att play.

Ye 16th.—A fayr day.   Shepheard continues very ill.   A messenger lay att ye anchor who pretends to be sent from Schomberg to discover deserters and those who hold correspondence wth ye enemy.   I was wth Mr. Fleetwood, Capt Clayton, and others att Clifton's.

Ye 17th.—A frost.   Birch continues to preach as ill as ever. Count Solmes came hither who landed last Thursday att Whithaven.   He came thither from Donnoghadee in 12 houres.   I saw Cunningham, who came along wth him, who sayes that Douglass has orders to Bombard Charlemont.   Sam Green came hither from Chester.

> The Rev. T. Birch "was constantly at variance with the High Church party and the local authorities" (Fishwick's History of the Parish of Preston).—Donaghadee is a seaport on the north-east coast of co. Down, 22 miles from Belfast.—Douglass was Lieut.-General Douglas.—Charlemont is a town in co. Armagh, about six miles north of the city of Armagh.

Ye 18th.—Early this morning Count Solmes went hence for London.   I went a coursing wth Mr. Fleetwood, Coll Rawstorn, and others.   Killed 5 hares, and din'd att Robins.

Ye 19th.—Mr. Hodgkinson had a letter from a private hand from London of ye ill state of affayres in Ireland.   We were invited there [Hodgkinson's] to dinner, wth Cousens Green and others, and after sup't att cousen Johnson's.   W. R. is ill of a sore eye.

> Mr. Hodgkinson would be Thomas Hodgkinson, late Alderman, of Preston.—W.R. may be meant for W.B., the diarist's cousin, William Bellingham, who was, two days afterwards, at Mr. Hodgkinson's.

Ye 20th.—A fayr day.   I walk'd to Camells to meete Bradley, but mist him.   I wrote to Kirkes officers and sent a present of tobacco.   I dranke wth little Dr. Parsons and Alderman Lemon.

Ye 21st.—A fayr day. I was all ye afternoone wth cousen Bellingham att Mr. Hodgkinson's. Fell ill att night of a feavour, and sent for Dr. Leigh.

Ye 22nd.—This day I was bled and vomited, and my feavour encreasd.

> From this date to the 13th of the following January there are no entries in the diary—evidently owing to indisposition—except one, which is in the form of a mem., as follows:—"Betty was born ye 12 of Dec., between 8 and 9 att night." She was the diarist's daughter Elizabeth, who died young.

January ye 13th, 1689/90.

Great frost and snow. This is the first day I went abroad [out of the house] since my sickness. I was att my cousen Johnson's and kindly treated, and att [? after] we treated them at our chamber.

Ye 14th.—Frost and snow. Cous Johns [Cousin Johnson] deliver'd of a dead child.

Ye 15th.—Frost and snow. Ye child buryd wth much formality.

Ye 16th.—Hard frost. My sister and her daughter supt att my chamber, on their own meat. This morning I discharg'd my Physitians. I went abroad and supt wth my sister.

> The sister and daughter were Mrs. Bickerton and her daughter Elizabeth.

Ye 17th.—Much frost and ye snow continues. I had some spitting of Blood when I cought [coughed]. Nabby has a very sore thum wch is mighty painfull.

Ye 18th.—Some snow. Ye frost continues and so does my paine and stiches in ye breast.

Ye 19th.—Frost continues. Nabby's much pain'd wth her thumb, and is sore afraid of a gangreene.

Ye 20th.—It begins to thaw. This afternoon I visited my cousen Patten. Nabby is in great paine.

Ye 21th.—The thaw continues. Nabby was in so great torture wth her thumb yt I sent for Doctor Tarlton, who apply'd pultices and oyntmt.

Ye 22th.—Nabby is still very ill. Harry fainted at ye sight of his mother's thumb. Nanny has a whitloe and was ill in her stomach.

Ye 23th.—A gentle thaw. I went to see ye children. Mr. Green and I witnessed a copy of ye Originall Articles—marriage between Simeon Pepper and Rose Lambert.

> Simeon Pepper of Ballygarth, co. Meath, married on the 15th of August, 1688, Rose, daughter of the Hon. Oliver Lambart, son of the first Earl of Cavan.

Ye 24th.—Some raine att night. Nabby has ease.

Ye 25th.—A very wett day. Mr. Stanley visited me.

Ye 26th.—A very fayr day. I was bled this morning by Dr Tarlton. Nabby had a sinew appeard att ye end of her thumb, att wch she was much discouraged.

Ye 27th.—A very warm day. I rode out in ye calash wth J. B. to ye Marsh to take ye air, and sup't and play'd att cards att Cous Johns[on's].

Ye 28th.—Some small raine. Rowley Singleton came hither from Leverpoole to goe to this school. I payd Mr Simeon Pepper some Breife money.

> Brief money is money obtained by a letter of authority, or from a collection authorised by a letter patent. The money which the diarist refers to was for the distressed Protestants of Ireland.

Ye 29th.—A warm day. I went wth Coll Rawstorne to Penwortham, and att night was entertain'd by Mrs. Langton wth Major Billings Guinea.

> The guinea had no doubt been won by Mrs. Langton from the Major while playing at some game—probably cards.

Ye 30th.—Much raine. Severall rode past, by this place [Preston], who left Ireland last Sunday, among whom was Lewt Norton of Devonshires Regiment. I supt att my sisters.

> "Last Sunday" was the 26th of January, so that the journey, by water and land, from Ireland to Preston, of the soldiers who "rode past," had occupied four days.

Ye 31th.—A fayr day. We have newes of ye Prorogation of ye Parlmnt to ye 2d of Apr, and yt ye King will goe in person for Ireland.

Feb ye 1st.

A very fayr day.

Ye 2d.—A cloudy, moist day. Ye Sacrament was administrd. There were severall Communicants, and I an unworthy one. Great preparations for Ireland.

Ye 3d.—A very fayr day. We supt and ended our Christmas att cousen Johnson's.

Ye 4th.—A fayr day. Little Betty had severall convulsions. My cousen Bellingham and I din'd att Penwortham.

> Little Betty was the child born on December 13th last, as mentioned in the diarist's memorandum.—The cousin alluded to was William Bellingham.

Ye 5th.—Little Betty continues very ill.   We had both Dr Lee and Parsons to her.   Ye Comrs [Commissioners] for ye ayd [? aid] mett here.

Ye 6th.—A wett day.   Ye child continues still very ill.

Ye 7th.—This morning between one and 2 the child dy'd : was bury'd about 6 in ye evening.

Ye 8th.—A very wett day.   My cousen B and I were most of ye afternoon att tables att Mr. Stanley's.

Ye 9th.—This day we had ye newes of ye dissolution of ye Parliament and a new one to be call'd ye 20th of march.   Mr. Birch preach'd a kind of a farewell sermon.

> Parliament was dissolved, by Proclamation, on the 2nd of this month.— The sermon may have appeared to be somewhat in the " farewell " category, but Mr. Birch continued Vicar of the church in which it was preached for about ten years longer.   Perhaps the " farewell sermon " had some reference to the old Parliament.

Ye 10th.—We went to Leverpoole, whence I sent some cloaths, etc., to J. White, by Dottinger.   There [at Liverpool] we stayd till ye 13th, which was a very wett day, and came home.   I receiv'd a letr from J. White : [it] was enclosed from Dublin.

> The part of this entry from " There we stayd " to the end of it must have been written on the evening of the 13th or some time next day.—J. White may have been related to Tom White previously mentioned, and at this time he was evidently in Ireland.—The " home " alluded to was at Preston, but it was only of a temporary character.

Feb. 14th.—A fayr day.   I discharg'd Mrs. Gregson for a quarters dyett.   Dr Wroe came to town this evening.   I supt wth him and Dr Leigh.

> A quarters dyett, i.e., a quarter's keep—food, &c.   Presumably the diarist arranged that the woman should leave his service for a money payment equivalent in value to a quarter's diet.—The two doctors were evidently friends.   Dr. Charles Leigh, to whose Natural History Wroe was a

subscriber, "speaks (i. 10) of some of his (Wroe's) experiments with mercury, alluding to him as ' our Learned Warden, the Rev. Dr. Wroe,' who had for several years kept ' an exact Diary of the Weather-glass '" (Palatine Note Book, in which there is a lengthy account—vol. 2, pp. 1—7—of Dr. Wroe's life and works).

Ye 16th.—A fayr day.   Mr. Bland preach'd 2 good sermons, on death.   Mr. Franks came home, and the Danish Quarter master wth him.

Ye 17th.—Severall of us went to Litham a coursing, and stayd there and had good diversion till ye 20th.   We came home and call'd att Westby mills.   This evening ye Ld Brandon came in here wth a great traine of ye militia officers and deputy Lewts of this county.

The greater part of this entry must have been made on the 20th or following day.—The district of Lytham has long been noted for its coursing facilities, and during the visit of the diarist there may have been a considerable gathering of gentlemen fond of the sport.   Many of the principal farmers about Lytham, in the old days, kept greyhounds for coursing purposes.   In the early part of last century there were coursing meetings of the " open " kind in the locality, and it is not improbable that they were established here a good many years further back.   Twice a year there are held in the Lytham district the important meetings of the Ridgway Coursing Club—a club founded in or about 1840, by the late Mr. Ridgway, of Bolton, &c., and some of his friends.—Between Lytham and Kirkham, at an elevated part, adjoining the road, there was formerly an old tavern called Westby Mills.   When this tavern was originally opened there may have been two or more wind mills in the neighbourhood—hence in all likelihood its name ; but in the latter days of the hostelry only one such mill stood near it.   The old tavern was pulled down in the fifties of last century, in Colonel Talbot Clifton's time, and on its site there was built a modernly arranged inn, called the Clifton Arms ; but the old name clings to the new place, which is much better known now as Westby Mills than the Clifton Arms. The site of this inn fronts the old Roman road known as Danes Pad, which in 1690, when the diarist was journeying here—indeed, almost down to 1790 —was the only " King's highway " from a very considerable portion of the Fylde to Preston : it ran from Westby by Ribby Hall, through Kirkham, past Clifton Mill, and so onward by Lea Town, across the ground now forming the course of the railway at Lea Road Station, to Ashton Four Lane Ends on the n.w.w. side of Preston ; so that Westby Mills would be definitely on the line of route, for the diarist, from Lytham to Preston.

The road which now runs from Ashton Four Lane Ends through Clifton village to the boundary of Newton-with-Scales was made by one of the de Hoghtons who had property in Clifton, &c. ; whilst that across the Marsh through Freckleton to Lytham was formed at a later time.   The wind mill which stood near the old tavern—Westby Mills—occupied the highest point in the district, and was reckoned one of the best " guides " on the west coast for mariners.   On a clear day it could be seen from the Irish sea for miles.   From the mill hill one of the most charming all-round views in England is commanded.   The Fylde of Lancashire is one of the old homes of English Catholicism, and Westby is one of its earliest homes in the Fylde (Our Country Churches and Chapels, pp. 345-6).   The wind mill was burnt down about 1875.

Ye 21th.—I heard ye Danish minister pray and preach.   Theyr service is very decent, and ye people very attentive.   They sing much and have their hands clasp'd and elevated.   I went wth Coll Carline to his lodgings, where we were treated wth Tea and coffee. In ye evening I was wth Sr Rich Standish, Coll Ashton, &c.

The Danish minister would be the chaplain to a number of Danish soldiers engaged to fight for William in Ireland, and the " people " alluded to would be a considerable portion of such soldiers, staying for a short time at Preston.   The army of William included soldiers from various countries. As to the Danes, a strong brigade of them was commanded, in Ireland, by Duke Charles Frederic of Wurtemberg.   " It was reported that of all the soldiers of William these were most dreaded by the Irish ; for centuries of Saxon domination had not effaced the recollection of the violence and cruelty of the Scandinavian sea kings ; and an ancient prophecy, that the Danes would one day destroy the children of the soil, was still repeated with superstitious horror " (Macaulay's History of England).—Colonel Carline was probably with the Danish contingent at Preston.

Ye 22th.—We have had fayr weather for this week.   Saw ye Danes exercise, and saw a Drummer putt to ye bastinado very severely.   I was wth Mr. Fleetwood and Mr. Spenser who intends to stand for Knight of ye Shire for this county.

Neither Mr. Fleetwood nor Mr. Spenser stood for knightship.

Ye 23th.—A fayr day.   Mr. Birch preach'd 2 dull sermons.   I was wth ye collonell of ye Danes.   We had newes of a victory at Newry.

Ye 24th.—We had no prayers though a Hollyday. Dr Tarlton came to town and Vice Chancellour Leighbourn. Nabby and I supt wth my sister.

> The Hollyday (holy day) was that of " St. Matthias the Apostle."

Ye 25th.—No prayers.   My cousen W. B. [William Bellingham] and I walk't to and dind att Penwortham.   I treated my Doctors and Shepheard att Corks.

> The names of the Doctors appear in previous entries.—Shepheard was in all probability the John Shepheard mentioned in the note under the entry for September 27th, 1689.

Ye 26th.—Some raine.   Chancery Court.   Mr Preston of Hooker [Holker Hall] came here, and assures us that Mr. Stanley and Holt will stand for ye Kts of ye Shire.   Edward Brandon Gerrard went hence to Ormskirk.

> Mr. Stanley stood for the position named, but Mr. Holt did not.—Edward Brandon Gerard was a Colonel of Foot, and a brother of Charles Gerard, created Lord Gerard of Brandon in 1645, and Earl of Macclesfield in 1679. His father was Sir Charles Gerard, Knt., of Halsall, co. Lancaster.

Ye 27th.—A fayr day.   We walk'd to Walton, and att night was treated att my sisters.   We had newes that Coll Wolseley had defeated a great party of ye Irish att Cavan and wounded ye Duke of Berwick.

> Colonel Wolseley—son of Sir Charles Wolseley, first baronet, a distinguished Statesman in the reigns of Charles I and Charles II—was the second baronet of Mount Arran, now Mount Wolseley, in co. Carlow, M.P. for the county town thereof, and an ancestor of the present Viscount Wolseley.—Cavan is the county town of co. Cavan.   The original town, supposed to have been an ancient one, was destroyed by fire in the attack made on it by the soldiers under Colonel Wolseley.

Ye 28th.—A sharp day.   I was wth Roger Kenyon.   Ye writts for electing Parliament men are gone from hence.   We have ye defeat att Dundalke confirm'd.   Alderman Percivall came here, and confirms ye newes of Wolseley's victory att Cavan. Ye like account ye Ld Brandon brought wth him.

> Lord Brandon would be Charles Gerard, eldest son of the before mentioned Earl of Macclesfield. He was a Colonel in the army.

March ye 1st.

Much raine last night and this morning. I was late att Cravens wth Mr. Fleetwood, Parker, Percivall, and severall others.

Ye 2d.—A fayr day. Ye Danes had ye Sacrament administred. They sing all theyr service, and differ from us in ye matter of Consubstantiation.

Ye 3d.—A hard frost. I was wth Ld Brandon at ye Coffee house. There were some few Cock matches. Mr. Dodwell came here from Yorkshire. Ye Danes exercised.

> Cock matches were cock fights.

Ye 4th.—A frost. Severall Cock matches. Sr Tho Stanly and Mr. Farrington had some difference about counting ye law. We had Major Billings and others drank att Crabtrees, where were most of ye gentlemen of ye town and ye Danish minister—a good scholar and ready in Latin. I spoake more Latin than I have done these 20 years. There are orders come for ye Danes to march. We supt att cousen Johns[on's]

> The difference had probably reference to counting the points in the fight, in accordance with the rules or law of such a contest.—Crabtree's place seems to have been a local inn or some large house wherein entertainment on a comprehensive scale could be obtained.

Ye 5th.—A frost and very fayr weather. I din'd att cousen Pattens. Cousen W. Bellingham went hence for Lancaster. Coll Rawstorne and I walk't wth Mrs Winkley and Mrs Francks as far as to ye boate.   Money came to pay ye Danes.   Att night one of them stabb'd young Wm Patten wth his bayonett att widdow Carrs.

> The two ladies named were the wives of gentlemen previously referred to. —The boat was that used at the ferry across the Ribble on the south side of Preston.—Young Patten would be the son of Henry Patten, and a grandson of the late Alderman Patten.—Widow Carr's would most likely be a tavern.

Ye 6th.—Much raine.   Ye Danes went hence towards theyr embarquing.   Some hopes are conceiv'd of W. Patten's recovery. I saw him dress'd.   Dr Tarlton came att night, wth cousen Patten, and has but small hopes.   This day ye election was att Lancaster. Coll [Roger] Kirkby and Mr [Thomas] Preston Chosen.

> The election of Members of Parliament or Knights of the Shire for the county of Lancaster, took place at Lancaster—anyhow, the result of the polling was officially declared there; but the election here mentioned by the diarist was for the borough of Lancaster.

Ye 7th.—A fayr day.   About 2 this morning young Patten dy'd.   Ye Coroner's inquest found it murder in both ye Danes. Ye town dispatch'd messengers wth ye account, to the coll and major, to Liverpoole.

> In the first instance, only one Dane appeared to have had a hand in the stabbing of young Patten; but the evidence given at the inquest implicated two.—The Mayor was, by virtue of his office, coroner for the borough, so that the messengers sent—at his request, no doubt—to the officers named would virtually be those of the town.

Ye 8th.—Lord Brandon came to town.   Young Patten was buryed.   Mr. Stanley, Earl of Derbyes brother, came hither.   He and Lord Brandon are to stand for Kts of ye Shire, none opposing them.   Sr Richard Standish and Mr [Peter] Shackerly are [candidates] for Wiggan.

> Mr. Stanley was the Hon. James Stanley, second son of the eighth Earl of Derby, and up to this time he had represented Clitheroe (1685) and Preston (1689) in the House of Commons.   He was a Whig.   Lord Brandon was also a Whig.—Sir R. Standish and Mr. Shackerley [usually spelt Shakerly] were elected members for Wigan.

Ye 9th.—A cold frost.   A second breife read for ye distress'd
Protestants of Ireland.   Mrs. Fleetwood dyed.

> Mrs. Fleetwood was the wife of Mr. Edward Fleetwood, of Penwortham.

Ye 10th.—A cold day.   Lord Brandon and Mr Stanly went to
Lancaster, in order to ye election.

Ye 11th.—A very fayr day.   I walk'd to Penwortham, to con-
dole Mr. Fleetwood for ye death of his Lady.   We hear that
severall vessells are gone wth ye Danes for Ireland.   God prosper
them.

Ye 12th.—Very fayr.   A monthly fast begins this day for
success to theyr matye's [Majestys'] forces in Ireland.   Madam
Fleetwood was this day bury'd att Penwortham.   Sr Rich Standish
gave me an account of the quarrell between Sr Edw Chisnell and
Mr. Shakerly.

Ye 13th.—Very fayr.   This day began ye election here [Preston].
Lord Willoughby, Mr. Rigby, Mr. Greenfeild, and Mr. Patten
candidates.   Mr. Rigby soone quitted his interests to ye Chancellour.   There were great heats [eagerness, excitement, &c.].   Ye
mobile [mob] struck ye Mayor, and twice confin'd him in ye town
hall.   Ye Court adjourn'd till to-morrow morning.   Mr. Pollard
and Mr. Nicholson came to this town.

> Lord Willoughby (de Eresby) was the eldest son of the third Earl of
> Lindsey, and held the office of Chancellor of the Duchy.—Mr. Rigby was
> Mr. Edward Rigby, presumably a son of Mr. Edward Rigby who was one of
> the M.P.'s for Preston from 1660 to 1681.—Mr. Greenfield was Christopher
> Greenfield, a local attorney-at-law.   In 1693 he was knighted.—Mr. Patten
> was Thomas Patten, son of the late Alderman Patten, and one of the
> representatives of Preston in the last Parliament.—The Court was the place
> in which votes were recorded.

Ye 14th.—Very fayr. Ye election continues. Still heat among ye rabble, which occasion'd the Courte to be adjourn'd to ye afternoone. all arts are us'd on both sides to procure votes : bed-ridd men are brought to ye Court. Att last ye Chancellor [Lord Willoughby] and Greenfeild carry'd it, and were declar'd. I walk'd wth Mr. Pollard, Mr. Hodgkinson, etc., to Walton, where we stay'd till ye noyse was over. I was after wth ye Recorder and ye vice Chancellor, and stayd out late.

> Lord Willoughby was a Whig; Mr. Greenfield was a Tory; and Mr. Patten, the defeated candidate, was a Whig. Mr. Patten petitioned against Lord Willoughby's election, on the ground—as alleged—that "The Mayor, Bailiffs, and Burgesses, to whom the precept was directed, had, by 'under practices,' procured many voters for his Lordship, and had polled several of them unqualified for that purpose, and had refused many qualified voters for the petitioner, and had returned the said Lord Willoughby in prejudice to the petitioner." An inquiry into the case, before a Committee of the House of Commons, took place, and the decision given confirmed the election of Lord Willoughby; but as his Lordship had in the meantime been called to the House of Peers, his seat at Preston became vacant, and a writ was ordered to be issued for an election there, so that the vacancy might be filled. Some time after his elevation to the House of Peers, Lord Willoughby was created Marquis of Lindsey and subsequently Duke of Ancaster and Kesteven. The election at Preston to fill the vacancy caused by the raising of Lord Willoughby to the Peerage took place on the 5th of December following. Sir Edward Chisenhall, Knt. (Tory), and Thomas Patten (Whig), who was defeated at the previous election, were the candidates. Sir Edward, who was a son of Colonel Edward Chisenhall and M.P. for Wigan in 1688, was elected by a majority of 57 votes.—The Recorder referred to was Mr. John Warren. He was the Recorder of Preston from 1684 till his death in 1706.

Ye 15th.—Some raine. Ye fayre was proclaimed. Att night I was wth Sr Edward Chisnell [Chisenhall], and visited Capt Neale who is sicke att Mr. Rishtons.

Ye 16th.—Storme and raine. We had an account of Scravenmore's being come from Bellfast to Chester. He sayes severall Danes were landed in Ireland before his coming away.

Ye 17th.—Some raine. Ye beast fair. I chargd Mr. Stanly wth what Mr. Livesey tould me, which he obstinately deny'd, and has promis't to disown it before company. We had some of Billinges token drunke att ye Talbott, where we were very merry and sate late.

> The token would be a "leaving token." Major Billings must have been on the point of leaving or have just left the town, and this was the manner in which he was " paying his way."

Ye 18th.—Moyst weather. Ye horse fayr. I had a bill from Mr. Chaddock of £5. I was wth Sr Edw Chisnell.

Ye 19th.—A fayr day. I walk't to and din'd att Penwortham. Was wth Mr. Hornby att ye Dogg.

Ye 20th.—A fayr day. This day ye Parliament meets att Westminster. I was to take leave of Mr. Greenfeild att night. I was wth Mr. Rishton of Antly and severall others of ye order of Montgomery, and consented to admits [admittance] of Dr Lee and Mr. Chaddock, they having pay'd for theyr contempt.

> Mr. Rishton would be Edward Rishton—a son of Geoffrey Rishton, M.D., of Antley Hall, near Accrington, who was one of the Parliamentary representatives of Preston from 1661 to the time of his death in January, 1666-67.—The order of Montgomery would be of a Masonic or cognate character. " Paid for theyr contempt " presumably means that the two persons named had paid some money as a penalty for neglecting, under-rating, or disrespecting the order or certain of its principles and requirements.

Ye 21th.—Fayr, dry, cold weather. Mr. Greenfeild went to London. We admitted Mr. Chaddock, Dr. Lee, and cous Johnson into ye order of Montgomery, by ye names of Mithridates, Hippocrates, and Memnon. There were at ye Chapter Lucius, Amphialus, Columbus, Scanderbegg, and my selfe, Cicero. Sr Tho Clifton had newes of his daughter Peters being deliver'd of a boy, and treated most of ye town att ye ale-house.

Ye 22th.—Dry weather. Mr. Bland came home. I gave him his wellcome to town. I sup't att my sisters.

Ye 23th.—Fayr weather. newes of a second defeat given att Cavan and Buttlers Bridge by Wolseley. Mr Chaddock payd his way going to Liverpoole.

> Butlers Bridge is a village four miles n.e. of Cavan.

Ye 24th.—Very fayr. I walk't wth ye women to Enam, and treated them att ye ale-house. Supt wth my sister.

1690.

Ye 25th [March].—Very fayr. A horse race at Penwortham, where Krichley's horse Beat Rigby's mare.

> The race would be run on Penwortham Marsh.

Ye 26th.—Very dry. I treated ye women att Enam. Cousen Patt[en] and Dolly were both in ye pets.

> In ye pets, i.e., in a displeased or sulky mood.

Ye 27th.—Very fayr. We walkt and din'd wth Mr. Crossan, near Whittle hills. Came to Dundee ale-house, and came home in good time. Mr. Chaddock return'd from Lerpoole.

> Mr. Crossan would be the Rev. Richard Croston, previously referred to. He was headmaster of Preston Grammar School from 1680 to 1689.—Whittle Hills are in the township of Whittle-le-Woods, about six miles south of Preston.—Dundee would be the alehouse sign-name.

Ye 28th.—Some showers. I was treated att Mr. Chaddocks, and were late wth Dr Wroe.

Ye 29th.—Moyst, growing weather. Cousen Johnson's brother Harry came to town. He is to be purser of the Pearl. Ye Mayor of Leverpoole came hither, and sayes that there are 4 French prizes taken by our ships, 2 of which are brought into Highleake [Hoylake], and yt Sr Cloud Shovel wth 9 ships are stood for the bay of Dublin.

> The Pearl was a warship carrying 56 guns (Berkley's Naval History of Great Britain).—The name of the Mayor of Liverpool for this year (1690) is not now known. There is no available list of Liverpool Mayors between 1688 and 1727.—Sir Cloudesley Shovel—a native of Norfolk, who entered the navy when thirteen years of age as a " gentleman volunteer "—was at this time a Vice-Admiral.

Ye 30th.—A fayr day. Harry Johnson went to Leverpoole. In ye evening ye High Sheriffe bold came to town. I sup't wth him, and sate upp late. Mr. Greenfeild came hither about 10 att night.

> The High Sheriff of Lancashire this year was Peter Bold, Esq., of Bold, between Warrington and Prescot.—Mr. Greenfeild was Christopher Greenfield, who was elected one of the Parliamentary members for Preston on the 14th of this month.

Ye 31th.—Some raine. We have an account yt Sr Clouy Shovels [Sir Cloudesley Shovel] wth a squadron of ships are come into Highleake [Hoylake]. Dr Wroe came to town, and I was wth him.

April ye 1st, 1690.

A very fayr day. I walk't to and din'd att Penwortham. We went to see some men fishing a marlepond, but gott little fish. They found a Hellmett in ye sluch. Captaine Parker came to us. He went wth us to the ale house. Nabby is very ill of ye tooth ach.

> Marlepond means a marl pit—a large hole, made through the excavation of marl, and containing water.—The Hellmett would be a helmet thrown by somebody—perhaps a deserter—into the pit.

Ye 2d.—A fayr day. Mr. Hilton came hither. He sayes all matters goe on well between ye K[ing] and Parl[iament]. We din'd att Cousen Johnson's.

> Mr. Hilton was probably the Hilton referred to on pp. xii. and 24, or a relative thereof.

Ye 3d.—A very fayr day. I visited Mr Bostock, who lies dangerously ill. I view'd ye lodgings att Tophams, and got a bill of £10 from Mr. Chaddock to be payd in London by Mr. flavell, merchs [merchant].

> Mr. Bostock was Richard Bostock, who was town's Bailiff at Preston in 1688-89.

Ye 4th.—A gloomy day. I was wth Mr. Farrington and Swetnam [? Swetenham]. Wrote severall letters. Was wth ye Mayor of lerpoole [Liverpool]. Wm Bellingham came to town. I was some time wth him, and was late wth ye Sherriffe. R. Bostock dy'd.

Ye 5th.—Windy weather. judge Ventris came in here this day, din'd att Mr. Pattens, and was treated wth a banquett by ye Mayor and town. Att night 2 Irish men, James Doran and Tho Bourke, were seiz'd as suspicious persons. They had letters about them to Sr James Poole, Sr Rowland Stanly, Sr Wm Creagh, and to young Mr. Mollineaux. They were examin'd aparte. They differ'd in theyr examinations and produc'd a counterfeite certificate under Rich. Engolsbys hand. They are secur'd and confin'd.

> Judge Ventris was Sir Peyton Ventris. He was a member of the Convention Parliament summoned by the Prince of Orange—was elected for the borough of Ipswich on January 12th, 1688-89. He resigned his seat in the same year on being made a Judge of the Common Pleas. After being thus raised to the Bench he was knighted. He was consulted by the Peers while the Corporations Restoration Bill, the Regency Bill, and other important legislative measures were in progress. On the 6th of April, 1691, he died (Nat. Dic. of Biog.).—Sir James Poole was probably related to the Poole family, of Poole Hall, in Cheshire.—Sir Rowland Stanley's family relationship and locale are of the shrouded order.—Sir William Creagh was, it is likely, the second son of William Creagh, who was ancestor of William Creag of Ballygarrett, co. Cork.—Young Mr. Mollineaux would be a son of Caryl, third Viscount Molyneux, who was made Lord-Lieutenant and Custos Rotulorum of the county of Lancaster by James II.

Ye 6th.—High western wind.   We had ye Kings letter and the statutes and Homily read in ye Church against Drunkenness. R. Bostock was buryed.

Ye 7th.—divers weathers.   I walk't wth Mr Green and Chaddoc[k]. One Edwards, a 3d person who was in company of Bourke and Doran, came to town and was examin'd.   He proves an honest man.   All theyr Portmanteaus were open'd and some letters were found, but of little consequence.

Ye 8th.—Very fayr.   I saw Loxam's horse heat att Penwortham marsh.   I din'd there, and saw a battle ragad between 4 cocks. Capt Clayton had a letter that gave an account how ill a condition K. Ja. army was in Ireland, and of 4 Regiments of French being landed there.

> Horse heat, i.e., a trial course or exercise.—Loxam would probably be John Loxam, a local Bailiff in 1693.—Ragad, i.e., raged—going on furiously.

Ye 9th.—Very fayr.   I walk'd to young Mr. Farringtons, and din'd there.   After went to ye ale-house in Lealand, and came home early.

> Young Mr. Farrington was William Farington (only surviving son of Henry Farington), of Worden Hall, near Leyland village, who was High Sheriff of Lancashire in 1714, and died without issue in the same year.

Ye 10th.—High wind.   I tooke Physick, wch wrought well.   I was visited by severall friendes.   Nabby walk'd wth Mrs. Gregson to Walton.

Ye 11th.—Storm and some showers.   This being ye anniversary of ye coronation of K Wm and Q Ma was kept here by ringing of ye bells, bonefires, etc.   Ye Mayor treated att Rattcliffes.   I began my steele course.

> Steele course—this means a course of chalybeate or tonic medicine.

Ye 12th.—High winds. I walk'd to see cous Johnson mare foal. We were wth Mr. Hodgkinson att ye ale[house], and sup't att my sister's.

Ye 13th.—Windy, but fayr. Coll Rawstorne had a letter from my Ld Brandon to keep ye Irish men close prisoners. Mr. Bland preach't an excellent [sermon], incentive to courage. Mr. Greenfeild pay'd his way.

Ye 14th.—Very fayr and warme. I was wth Major Noell. Mr. Greenfeild and Sudall went to London.

> Sudall would be Alderman Roger Sudell, who was Mayor of Preston in 1681-2 (Guild year), 1690-1, 1699-1700, and 1707-8.

Ye 15th.—Very fayr. I saw ye horse heat—9 minutes 4 mile. I walk'd to Walton wth Dr Lee, and after view'd Burkell's engine for great guns to approach wthout danger of ye engineers. Mr Chaddock came home and tell us that ye Dover and St. Albans came into Highlake and brought 2 prizes taken off Ireland wth some officers and soldiers.

> The Dover was a ship of war, but not one of the first order. In the list of cruisers for 1696 her name appears, and she is subsequently mentioned amongst "some Ships that have done Service by Cruising," her achievements as specified under this head being the re-taking of an English ship and the capture of a French privateer. The St. Albans was a warship of 50 guns, and she was amongst the ships, commanded by Admiral Russell, which fought the French fleet, off La Hogue, in 1692 (Berkley's Naval History of Great Britain).

Ye 16th.—fyne wth some small showers. Ye monthly fast very solemnly observ'd. Mr Langton came from Lerpoole and brought a letter from Bell of Dublin to ald: Squire

> Alderman Squire would be a Liverpool gentleman.

Ye 17th.—fayr but windy. I went to meete Mr. Fleetwood att ye marsh. Coll Matthews came to town. Cous [Sam] Green had a quarrell wth one Attkinson belonging to the navy. Words and blows happen'd and a great uproar was made. He [? Col. Matthewes] tooke them before a magistrate. It is thought Sam Green was in drinke.

Ye 18th.—Very fayr. I went wth Coll Matthewes to see Dore [? Doran] and Bourke. These Irishmen were taken att Lodge and att ye ashes and brought to town. I treated Collonell Matthewes att George Rattcliffes. Ye Sacramt adminstred.

> There is a hamlet called Lodge, near Settle, in the West Riding of Yorkshire; but it is exceedingly improbable that this was the place referred to. It may fairly be presumed that Lodge was what used to be known as "The Lodge," in Myerscough, about seven miles n.n.w. of Preston—a seat of the Tyldesleys, who were strong supporters of the Stuart dynasty. One of them (Thomas) was the owner and occasional occupier of the Lodge at the time when the diarist, Colonel Bellingham, was at Preston. This Thomas was a Roman Catholic and an ardent Jacobite, as was also his son Edward, who joined the followers of the first Pretender, at Lancaster, in 1715.—The name "ashes" relates to Ashes, in Goosnargh, about nine miles n.n.e. of Preston—the old residence of a noted Roman Catholic family named Threlfall, one of whose members (Edmund) was on intimate terms with Thomas Tyldesley of The Lodge, in Myerscough, and a very active plotter against William III.

Ye 19th.—Very fayr. A Dutch troop came to town. I was a little time wth Mr Farrington and others. I went to visit Dore [? Doran], and found a Dutch trooper wth him, on whose toe he had trod when I came in.

> The toe would be trod on, or pressed, as a hint to be reticent, or cautious in speaking.

Ye 20th.—Very fayr. Very many Communicants (God be praysed). Mr. Bland made a very good sermon in ye afternoon. I walk't wth Nabby a good while in Enam Garden. I sent a token to D. Bickerton.

> D. (Daniel) Bickerton was a nephew—a son of Robert Bickerton, who married the diarist's sister.

Ye 21th.—Still very fyne. One Dodsworth, a person who pretends to discover a plott of ye Papists, is come to this town. He insists much upon having money before he informes. I was wth Coll Matthewes, Major Longworth, etc., att Rattcliffes, and was in ye evening att Enam, where my cousen W. B. treated ye women.

Ye 22th.—Very fayr. Ye Dutch troop sent out a party to apprehend Papists, and brought in one Irish man, who had his wife wth him. In ye evening we had a bowl of Punch att ye mitre.

Ye 23th.—Some showers towards evening. This day severall of ye gentlemen had a very good dinner att ye marsh, and bowld in ye afternoon. We had an account by one come from Chester that Sr Clouds [Cloudesley] Shovell went into Dublin bay wth ye mounthmoth [? Monmouth] yatcht and his own pinnace, and brought thence a man of warr of 25 guns.

Ye 24th.—Very fayr. In ye afternoon Cous W. B. and W. P. and I treated ye women att Walton.

The cousins were William Bellingham and William Patten.

Ye 25th.—Very fayr. I went wth W. B. and W. P. to see Major Farrington, who lyes very ill of ye gout and stone. He tould us he had Beere of nine yeares old. We call'd on Mr. Dandy, and we came home, where W. B. and I saw a very comicall sight.

Ye 26th.—Very fayr. I din'd wth Mr. Fleetwood and Coll Matthewes att Coll Rawstornes, where we were handsomely entertain'd, and after dinner were very merry att Rattliffs.

Ye 27th.—Very hott weather. Mr. Gregory preach't twice, and [I] was att Church both times. Coll Matthewes in the evening. Nabby and I tooke a long walke. We had an acct by this dayes newes of great clashing in the house of Commons and [that] it came to drawing of swords.

Ye 28th.—Very fyn, but somewhat windy. Great cocking att Graystocks. I din'd wth Coll Matthewes att cous Johnsons. Mr. Luke King and Mr. Frankes came from London.

> Graystocks would be a portion of Graystock Brow—some fields about a mile from Preston, on the n.w. side.—Some years after this entry was made there was a Mr. Luke King residing at Worsewell, in Cheshire; he qualified as a burgess of Preston at the Guild in 1702; and he may have been the person mentioned, or a descendant.

Ye 29th.—Very much raine about mid night and some showers in ye morning. I din'd wth Sr Edw Chisnall [Chisenhall], who came here to stand for Burgess in the roome of ye Ld Willoughby, who is call'd to ye house of Lords. I went to ye marsh a cocking, and after was late wth Sr Edw Chisnall and Luke King.

Ye 30th.—Very much raine most of this day. Sir Edw Chis went hence. I wrote [sent a letter] by Campbell to Ireland, and was in ye evening wth Cous B and Coll Rawstor[ne].

May ye 1st.

Some showers. Ye Quarter sessions was held here. Mr. Stanly is continued on his Recognizance. I was att play wth Mr. King, and att evening was wth ye Justices att Rattliffes. Threllford escap'd.

> Threllford may be intended for Threlfall. Nearly a year prior to this a warrant was issued for the apprehension of Edmund Threlfall, of Ashes, in Goosnargh, who had been a keen conspirer against William III; but he kept evading it, and successfully persisted in this course until his death, which

occurred through wounds he received whilst resisting some militiamen, evidently on the look-out for him, near Ashes, in August, 1690. It is not improbable that the Threllford mentioned by the diarist was this same Edmund Threlfall.

Ye 2d.—Very fayr. I saw Mr. Suddell who is return'd from London. I was att play most of ye evening wth Mr. King, who is fallen very ill, and was late wth Coll Matthewes and others att Rattliffes.

Ye 3d.—Very good growing weather. A soldier who came late from Ireland tould us of some action att Charlemont, where 30 of ye enemy were killed and 25 taken prisoners, wth ye loss only of 7 of our side, and that Tirconnell was in disgrace with K J [King James]. Coll Matt:[hewes] gave us a noble treat att ye anchor. Capt Poultny came in just as we were at supper.

Ye 4th.—A fayr day. Coll Matthewes and Capt Poultney went hence. I receiv'd a large mapp wth some verses from Greenfeild. Ye mapp is of Ireland, and ye verses an anniversary song, made by Durfy, on ye Q[ueen's] birthday, being ye 30th of apr.

> Durfy was Thomas D'Urfey, dramatist and song writer, who was of Huguenot descent, born at Exeter, in 1653, and a nephew of Honoré d'Urfé, who wrote the notable romance of Astrée.

Ye 5th.—Some raine. I walk't and din'd wth Mr. King, att Penwortham, and was on att night wth Tom Ashton, who payd his way att ye dogg.

> Tom Ashton was a gentleman who resided at Littlewood, a hamlet in the parish of Croston, about seven miles s.w. of Preston.

Ye 6th.—Much raine. We have newes of recruits being gotten into Charlemont. I saw one Buchanan who was a minister att Clogher in Ireland.

Ye 7th.—A very fayr day. Severall of us din'd att ye Marsh. I bowl'd most of ye day, and when I came home I went wth Mr. Mollineaux to Rattliffs. Sr Edw Chisnall came to us.

Ye 8th.—Very fayr. I was handsomely treated by Sr Ed Chisnell att ye anchor. Here was Capt Pash and Corpr [? Capt] Berry of Sr George St. George Regiment. They are sent wth private orders relating to Papists. I was late wth them and wth Sr Ed Chis.

Ye 9th.—Very fayr. Sr Edw Chisnall treated ye Mayor, Aldermen, and Common Councell, att ye anchor. Coll Rawstorne and his Lady came to visitt us. I heard of H. Bickertons misfortune, and was att night wth Sr Ed Chisnall.

Henry Bickerton was another nephew of the Diarist; he died in 1740.

Ye 10th.—Very fayr. Dr Wroe came hither. I was wth him. I bought some wheat to send for Ireland. Sr Edw Chisnall went hence.

Ye 11th.—Very fayr. Ye Vicar preach'd. In ye afternoone I walk'd to Penwortham wth Mr King, Winkly, and Frankes.

Ye 12th.—Very fayr. This day we remov'd into ye Friargate, to Evan Hewson's house. I putt 2 sacks of wheat on board ye may flower to send to Ireland.

Friargate, in Preston, now mainly contains shops; but when this entry was made it was a thoroughfare of a considerably residential character.—Evan Hewson or Hughson was the town's Bailiff for the municipal year 1681-2; in 1683 he was elected a member of the Common Council; and he continued to be a member of this body for many years.—The May Flower would be a coasting vessel, and the sacks of wheat would be put on board at a small pier or quay, by the side of the Ribble, near the west corner of Preston Marsh.

Ye 13th.—Very fayr.   Cousen W. B. went wth me to ye vessell.

The vessel would be the May Flower.

Ye 14th.—Very fayr.   I putt some brandy and biskett, etc., on board, and bowl'd att ye Marsh in ye afternoon.

Ye 15th.—Very fayr.   We were treated att Gradells.

Graddells—no doubt Thomas Gradwell's. He was the town's Bailiff in 1691-2.

Ye 16th.—Still fayr.   I went and tooke leave att Penwortham.

At Mr. Fleetwood's, &c.

Ye 17th.—Very fayr, but sharp and windy.   I tooke leave of severall in ye town.   Cousen Johnson visited us.   I was wth Sr Wm Penington and Mr. Fleetwood.   Betty was very ill last night.

The town was, of course, Preston.

Ye 18th.—Still fayr.   We had an account from Lerpoole of Lewt King's deserting K James and coming over wth a list of ye Irish army.   He sayes that Charlemont has capitulated to surrender.   I bought my gray horse from Jean, at boat house, for £7 10s.

Ye 19th.—Very fayr.   Mr. Greenes child christened.   My sister treated Mr. King and us att dinner.   We were very merry, and late att George Rattliffes, and sung att ye high cross.

The High Cross was in the centre of the Market Place.

Ye 20th.—Very fayr.   I was att Marsh bowling, and att night treated severall friendes wth Punch att my chamber.

May y 23th 1690

very windy, we vowld, Martin y Attorney came in a
Gabbard from Dublin, he gave an accu of my freinds
but was very reserved to y mayor.
y 24th

much wind and raine, Giles had his legg broken Dr
Reinmond and severall freindes were with us.
y 25th

much raine, a funerall sermon on Hughes of Dublin
a goldsmith, Dr Guithers was with us
y 26th

some raine, we went to High Lake, went to Capt.
Greenhill for an order for our horses, was on
board y Ruby and returnid to Leverpoole.
y 27th

much raine, mr Long and I came to Hyle Lake,
we dind with mr Vickars, came to Wallery to Johns
in y Quakers, where we nett, Cremer, Joffers, Pearson
and Killcock, my man came to us at 12 att night
with an order to shipp our horses.
y 28th

raine in y morning, we went to Hyle Lake and
shipt our horses early, and sayled about 3 in y after
noon, we came att night in sight of Ilk of Man,
our ship y Betty of Biddiford, Tho Marshall mr.
y 29th

a fayr Gale in y morning, but calme about noon
all day & rest of y day, near y Mull of Galloway
and att evening came to an Anchor near y Cope
land Islands

FACSIMILE OF A PAGE OF THE BELLINGHAM DIARY.

Ye 21th.—Much raine. Ye fast day. Mr. Bland preach'd a very good sermon, but fell very ill of his legg. I was wth Coll Rawstorne and others att Rattliffes.

Ye 22th.—A fayr day. I came to Leverpoole wth cousen W. B. [William Bellingham] and Mr. King. We had ye assurance of ye surrender of Charlemont and Woolselye's action att Ballingargy. Ye Pinnace of ye monk was lost wth ye Lewt and 12 men. I saw Winkworth who made escape from Dublin in apr[il].

> Woolselye was Captain Richard Wolseley, M.P. for Carlow.—Ballingargy is intended for Ballingarry, in co. Limerick.—The Monk was a warship of 60 guns.—Lewt. means Lieutenant.

Ye 23th.—Very windy. We bowl'd. Martyn ye Attourny came in a Gabbard from Dublin. He gave an acct: of my freindes, but was very reserv'd to ye Mayor.

> A gabbard is a sailing vessel intended for inland navigation—a barge or lighter.

Ye 24th.—Much wind and raine. Giles had his legg broken. Dr Richmond and severall freindes were wth us.

Ye 25th.—Much raine. A funerall sermon over Hughes of Dublin, a goldsmith. Dr. Guithers was wth us.

Ye 26th.—Some raine. We went to Highlake [Hoylake]. Went to Capt Greenhill for an order for our horses. Was on board ye Ruby, and return'd to Leverpoole.

> The Ruby was a war vessel of 50 guns.

Ye 27th.—Much raine. Mr. King and I came to Hyle lake [Hoylake]. We din'd wth Mr. Vickars. Came to Wallesy, to John in ye Gutters, where we mett Cremer, Foster, Person, and

Allcock. My man came to us att 12 att night wth an order to shipp our horses.

Wallesy, i.e., Wallasey, is in Cheshire, four miles n. of Birkenhead.— John in ye Gutters was presumably either a jovial friend bearing this soubriquet or the name of an inn.

Ye 28th.—Raine in ye morning. We went to Hyle lake [Hoylake], and shipt our horses early, and sayld about 3 in ye afternoon. We came att night in sight of Isle of Man. Our ship ye Betty of Biddiford [Bideford] ; Tho: Marshall mr [master]

Ye 29th.—A fayr day. Gale in ye morning, but calm about nine. We lay most of ye day near ye Mull of Galloway, and att evening came to an Anchor near ye Copeland Islands.

Ye 30th.—Some showers. About 3 this morning we came to an anchor att ye Whitehouse. I went wth Mr. King to Carrigfergus. Saw Dean Ward, and Mr. King heard yt Kirke was displeased att him. About 12 I came by boat to Belfast. Din'd att Mr. Carbuy's, sup't wth Mr. Twigg, and lay that night wth him. I wrote to Nabby.

Ye 31th.—Some raine. I came to Lisburn : waited on Ma. Gen. Kirk. Was wth ye Duke, who was very obleiging. I din'd wth ye Earl of Meath, and came to Jo. Whites.

Lisburn is a town in co. Antrim, seven miles s.s.w. of Belfast.

June ye 1st.

Much raine. I went to Magherelin ; heard Mr. Cubbidge preach ; Din'd att his house wth ye Coll of the Brandenburgh Regiment ; and was after with major Williams and Capt Brereton att Mrs. Kellys. Ye Ld Drogheda passt by.

Magherelin, i.e., Magheralin, is a parish partly in co. Armagh and partly in co. Down, two miles s.w. of Moira.—Mr. Cubbidge was a Protestant minister at Magheralin.

Ye 2d.—Severall showers. Some Quakers came to see me. I walk'd in ye afternoon to Moyragh, saw Sr Arthur Rawden's house, and walk'd wth Capt Ross to ye conservatory. The house and much of ye goods are well preserv'd.

> Moyragh, i.e., Moira, is in co. Down, about 14 miles s.w. of Belfast.

Ye 3d.—A fayr day. I went to ye mill. In ye afternoon I went to Drummond, and was treated by Capt Brereton.

> The mill would be one for flax or corn.—Drummond was, presumably, at this time the name of a very small place, or residence, not far from Magheralin.

Ye 4th.—A fayr morning ; some showers in ye afternoon. I went to Lisbourn, waited on M G Kirke, delivered him his letter, din'd wth Mr. Aleway, and was wth ye Duke. Some French horse came in. I saw cousen Purcell. I wrote to Nabby and Dan by ye poast, and came home in good time.

> Dan, i.e., Daniel Bickerton.

Ye 5th.—Abundance of raine. J. Shepheard came hither, and brought newes of ye K leaving London yesterday.

> The King was, of course, William III.—The " newes " was quite correct, and, considering the distance, it had somehow come with marvellous rapidity. But, perhaps, Shepheard was only mentioning a rumour he had heard, some time before coming, to the effect that the King intended to leave London on a certain day which corresponded, when he reached where the diarist was located, with " yesterday."

Ye 6th.—High wind and some showers. Shepheard stayes still here. We have an account of a prey being taken by ye soldiers of Bellturbet, and parte of them brought into these [? their] quarters to be sold.

> Prey, i.e., goods, &c., taken by force—booty, plunder.—Belturbet is a town about nine miles n. of Cavan.

Ye 7th.—Wind and some showers. Shepheard went hence this morning. We hear ye enemy are advancing.

Ye 8th.—Very much raine. I receiv'd ye Sacram[ent] att Macherelin [? Magheralin], where Mr. Cubbidge preach'd a very suitable sermon for ye day. I din'd wth him, and was wth Mr. John Disney. Capt Lowry came hither and stayd all night.

Ye 9th.—Still wett weather. Lowry went hence this morning. I design'd for Hillsborough, but ye raine prevented me. John White payd Gillett his rent for grassing.

> Design'd, i.e., intended.—Hillsborough is a town in co. Down, about 10 miles s.w. of Belfast.—For grassing, i.e., for the privilege of using certain land on which to spread out flax, &c., for bleaching, or for grazing cattle, or getting turf. The land thus used was probably in the parish of Gernonstown, near the diarist's burnt residence.

Ye 10th.—A fayr day. I went to Lisbourn, but ye D[uke] was gone to Bellfast, thinking to meete ye K[ing], but return'd. I came wth Capt Ponell [Pownell], and stayd some time with Mr. Moore, att Hillsborough, wch is preparing for ye King's reception. Yt night there were severall bonefires made, in believing ye K was landed ; but it proved an ignis fatuus. Severall Regiments are on theyr march towards ye rendezvous near Ardmagh and Legathory. C: G: Douglas commands them.

> Ardmagh means the city of Armagh, the latter name being a contraction of the former, which signifies a high field or high place.—Legathory would be a small place not far from Armagh.—The regiments referred to would be mainly, if not entirely, Scotch ones.—Evelyn in his diary refers to General Douglas. Under date February 19th, 1689-90, he says :—" I din'd with the Marquis of Carmarthen (late Lord Danby), where was Lieutenant-General Douglas, a very considerate and sober commander, going for Ireland. He related to us the exceeding neglect of the English soldiers, suffering severely for want of cloaths and necessaries this Winter, exceedingly magnifying their courage and bravery during all their hardships."

Ye 11th.—A very hott day. We wash'd our sheep. I din'd wth Capt Ponel att Drummore [Dromore]. Some French challeng'd some horses in theyr parkes, but ye Major and Capt Ponell sent them to ye gaurd. There were more bonefires made this night.

> The sheep may have been the diarist's own, or perhaps they were for the commissariat department.—The challenge probably means that the French claimed (an old meaning of the word challenge) some horses in the enclosures set apart for baggage, horses, stores, &c.—The bonfires would be to celebrate the supposed arrival of King William at Carrickfergus.

Ye 12th.—Very hott. I went to Moyragh [Moira] and saw Jewells Regiment of horse, wch is a very good one ; but ye Danish Regiment of gaurds is ye best I ever saw. They are [? have] an orange colour'd livery fac'd wth crimson velvett. I din'd att Moyragh, and saw Mr. Sheenes, Capt Hamilton, and Lewt Hamilton who was at Gernongtowne [Gernonstown]. Eben Loe was wth me.

Ye 13th.—Very hott. I went to Moyragh to see one Hatch, who came a weeke agoe from Drogheda. He call'd att Gernonstowne, and says things are very well there, and that there is much corne growing thereabouts. He sayes K James his army is in an ill condition for want of most necessaryes. There are about 7000 of them encamp'd near Ardee. There are 3 regiments in Dundalk and 3 in Drogheda, to wch they have added no fortifications more than what were last summer. I saw Capt Wm Ponsonby att Moyragh and Lewt Coll Petrie.

Ye 14th.—A great shower of raine after dinner, about wch time we fancyd we heard some great Guns off, from Bellfast, wch we hope are for ye K[ing] landing. Here came James Hunter, ye Quaker, and a quarter master of Levison's dragoons. Ye K landed at Carricfergus.

> " When King William III, preparing to invade Ireland, made inquiries as to the best ports at which to get shipping for his troops, he was told by the Customs officials that Chester had no ships and only a few small barks for

coasting trade, while Liverpool had ' 60 or 70 good ships of 50 to 200 tons.'
But the officials were doubtful if much use could be made, ' because they
drive a universal foreign trade to the Plantations (colonies) and elsewhere,'
and were continuously engaged.   The business of transport was now
despised by Liverpool shipowners, and the terms they charged were so high
that the royal officials were frightened and applied for further instructions ''
(Muir's History of Liverpool, p. 138).   The instructions did not favour
embarkation from Liverpool.

Ye 15th.—A fayr day.   I went to church, and din'd wth Mr
Cubbidge.   Heyfords dragoons are quarter'd att Macharelin
[Magheralin].

Ye 16th.—A hott, close day.   I was sent for by 2 this morning,
and before 6 I came to Bellfast.   I was kindly receiv'd by ye
D[uke] and Kirke, and favourably recommended to ye K[ing],
whose hand I kiss't, and he promis'd to remember me.   I was most
of ye afternoone wth ye secretary.   Ye K road out in ye evening.
I lay wth Mr. Mason.   This day wrote letters for England, to
Nabby, etc.

Ye 17th.—A hott day.   I gave ye K a petition.   Din'd att
Rourk's wth Mr. Neway and others, and came home late.   We
mett wth some French thieves.

   The thieves would probably be a few pillaging French soldiers belonging
to the French regiments in the service of William III.

Ye 18th.—Very hott.   I sent Art away early this morning wth
letters.   I had an answer from Toby Purcell.   Mr. Loe was here.

Ye 19th.—Very hott.   I walk'd to ye mill and wash'd there.

Ye 20th.—Very great showers.   I went to Hillborough.   Saw
ye K and drank of his wine.   A messenger came in from ye Ld
Dover to desire a leave to transport himselfe and family to Ostend.

2 dragoons were brought in prisoners. I was wth my Ld Meath and Mr. Neway att theyr tents, and brought Hunter ye Quaker's wife behind me home.

> This means that they went home together on one horse—she riding pillion fashion, i.e., on a pad or cushion connected with the rear part of the saddle.

Ye 21th.—A fayr day. I went to view ye camps att Drumore [Dromore]. I saw Mr Render and mrs. Kingswell. An express to ye K from Kirke. I call'd att Count Menard's Regiment ; saw ye Bankers and some of ye officers. I road some way wth my Lord Berkely. He assures me ye King marches tomorrow. There are orders come out for 500 labourers to goe to ye Newry to assist ye Pioneers in levelling the roads.

> Lord Berkely was Charles, summoned to Parliament as Lord Berkeley in the lifetime of his father, succeeded him as second Earl, and was appointed one of the Lord Justices of Ireland in 1699.

Ye 22th.—A hott day. This morning we had a skirmish wth ye enemy about Moyragh pass, wherein we lost above 20 men, but kill'd more of ye enemy. I waited on Sr Ar Rawden att Moyragh, and sup't wth Coll Matthewes, who has gotten Heyfords Regiment.

> Sir Arthur Rawden was the eldest surviving son of Sir George Rawdon (only son of Francis Rawdon, Esq., of Rawdon, in the West Riding of Yorkshire), who settled in Ireland, was a military commander during the rebellion in that country in 1641, and subsequently took an interest in various Irish affairs till his death, in 1684.

Ye 23th.—Very hott. I rode out to Macherelin and Moyragh, and stayd some time wth Sr Ar Rawden.

Ye 24th.—fayr but windy. Last night I fell very ill, and this morning took Cardmis [? Carduus] possett and was better. I had an account from one Wood, who wrought att ye highway, that ye King was as far as Moyragh pass, and yt there were found much more of ye enemy than of our men dead upon ye place. Art return'd this evening to our great satisfaction, wth whom I immediately went to ye King att Loghbricklan [Loughbrickland]. I was kindly receivd by severall of ye Nobility. I was for some time in private wth ye Earl of Portland and Secretary of State. Ye acct [account or report] was very full and very satisfactory. I lay wth Mr. Mason and wrote [sent] letters to Nabby by an express. There was great shooting towards Carling[ford].

> Carlingford is about 20 miles, measured in a direct line, south of Loughbrickland.

Ye 25th.—Very fayr, but windy. I was for some time this morning wth ye Secretary. Came home about 12 o'clock, and was preparing for my march to-morrow.

> Home simply means here a temporary sojourning place, and it would be either at Moira or a little south thereof.

Ye 26th.—Very hott. K march'd to Newry, where I saw my brother Rochfort att To Purcells. I waited on ye Genrll. We encamp'd on ye s side of Newry.

> Rochfort was Robert Rochfort, the diarist's brother-in-law. He married Hannah Handcock, sister of Mrs. Bellingham. In a note on p. 2 some reference is made to him.

Ye 27th.—Very hott. About 2 this morning I mov'd towards Dundalk, and entrd it about 6 wth Lewt Gennll Solmes and M. G. Kirke. Ye towne is wholy deserted, but strongly fortify'd. No inhabitants left but Capt Bolton and his wife, who are both stript. Our army encamp'd about a mile south from Dundalke, being now entire, Douglas party having joyn'd ours. J. White and I went as farr as Lurgan race, and sate there some time eating bread and cheese.

> A race, of the sort here referred to, is a strong, quick-flowing current of water, or the channel for such-like current, or a water-course above a dam to a water wheel.

BELLINGHAM FAMILY HEIRLOOMS.

Amongst these are the above, viz., the Colonel's Diary, Liqueur Case given to the Colonel by William III, and knife, fork, and spoon, used by William III on the day before the Battle of the Boyne.

Ye 27th [supplementary entry].—The K[ing] resolv'd to attack ye enemy this night in their quarters att R D [Ardee]; but, hearing by some Dragoons who were att ye very gate, and kill'd 2 of theyr men there, yt ye enemy are retir'd, he putt off his resolution.   I waited on ye K att supper, and where he discours'd me most of ye time, and was extreamly pleasant and cheerfull.   I wrote to England.

> Ardee is about 12 miles s.w. of Dundalk.

Ye 28th.—Very hott.   I waited on ye King to Ardee.   From thence was ordered by him to goe wth Ginkell and Camboon to view all the river for encamping.   We went as farr as Cappock bridge, and so return'd to our camp near Dundalk.   I stay'd some time by ye way att Gernonstown, and found severall of the tenants wth theyr cattle had stayd att home att my instance.   I found little Jenny very well.   Ye enemy are retird beyond Boyn.

> Ginkell (created Earl of Athlone by William III) was one of the Generals.
> —Camboon was Colonel Cambon, an officer of much repute.—Cappock
> Bridge is in Cappoge or Kippogue, a parish in the barony of Ardee, not far
> from Dunlee on the river White.

Ye 29th.—Excessive hott.   I was very early this morning wth Gennll Ginkell, who gave orders to Coll Matthewes to let me have what dragoons I wanted for ye security of my tenants and theyr cattle.   I march'd wth Coll Matthewes, and came to Gernonstowne about 6 in ye morning.   He left me Quarter-master Cowly and 6 dragoons.   Ye traine of Artillery and a great parte of our army march'd our road.   My brother Rochfort lay wth me this night. I took upp some money which lay hidden for some time.

Ye 30th.—Very hott.   I call'd at Mr. Townley's in our march towards Boyn.   I was some time wth ye King on ye hill of Tullaheskar, from where he view'd Drogheda, and then went towards Old bridge.   On ye S side of Boyn lay ye enemyes camp, which, ye King going to view, he was hitt by a cannon shot on his shoulder, wch putt us into the greatest consternation imaginable ; but, blessed be God, it proved but a slight hurte.   He went round his own camp, and was receiv'd wth ye greatest joy and acclamations imaginable.   Ye cannon fir'd att each all ye afternoone.   We drew a great body of our horse upp on ye hills each side of ye enemy.   We fir'd severall Bombs, some of which did execution, and our cannon dismounted 2 of ye enemyes batteryes.

Mr. Townley's was Townley Hall, three miles from Drogheda.   It has been the family seat of the Balfours for over 200 years.   The present occupant is Blany Townley Balfour, D.L.—Tullaheskar should be Tullyesker.   The hill is on the north side of, and about two and a half miles from, Drogheda.   It is in co. Louth.—Oldbridge is on the right bank of the river Boyne, three miles n.w. of Drogheda.

July 1st, 1690.

A joyful day.   Excessive hott.   About 6 this morning ye King gott on horseback and gave ye necessary orders.   Kirke order'd me to bring him some account from ye enemy.   I brought him a youth, one Fyans, who came that morning from Drogheda.   I carry'd him to ye King, who was then standing att ye Battery, seeing his cannon play att ye house of Old bridge.   He had sent early a strong detachment of about 15,000 men, wth Douglass, towards Slane, who pass'd ye river wthout any opposition, and putt ye enemy to rout who were on that wing.   He sent another detachment of horse to ye left, to goe over att ye mill foord ; but, ye tide coming in and ye foord bad, ye passage was very difficult, most of them being forc'd to swim, insomuch that they could not come upp time enough to assist our foot, who went over ye foord att Old bridge about 11 of ye clock.   Ye enemy had layd an ambush behind ye ditches and houses on ye other side of ye water, who fir'd incessantly att our men as they were passing the river, who as soon as arriv'd on land immediately putt those musqueteers to ye rout and advanc'd farther into ye feild in Battalia [battalion]. Here ye brave old Duke Schomberg was kill'd and Dr Walker and Coll Callincott mortally wounded. Ye enemy advanc'd towards us and made brisk effort upon us ; but we soone repell'd them wth considerable loss on theyr side. They made 2 other attempts upon us ; but were still bravely beaten back ; and when our horse of ye left came upp ye enemy quite quitted that feild, having left severall dead bodyes behind them. 'Twas there we tooke Lewt Gennll Hamilton. Ye enemyes horse of Tirconnell's Regiment behav'd themselves well, but our Dutch like angells. Ye K[ing] chargd in person att ye head of ye Eniskilliners, and expos'd himselfe wth undaunted bravery. He pursu'd allmost as farr as ye Naul, and left them not till near 10 a clock att night. I was his guide back to Duleeke. We kill'd about 2000 of theyr men, besides Ld Carlingford, Dangan, and severall other officers of noate kill'd and taken prisoners. We lost not above 200 in ye whole action, many of which were kill'd by our own men through mistake. I return'd to ye camp att Old bridge, having left ye King in his coach att Duleeke, where he stay'd that night. I was almost fainte for want of drink and meat.

Lord Carlingford—Nicholas, the second Earl of Carlingford and third Viscount Taaffe—had command of a regiment of foot which fought on the side of James II at the battle of the Boyne. He was succeeded in titles, &c., by his brother Francis, "the celebrated Count Taaffe of the Germanic Empire." Francis was so much esteemed by most of the European crowned heads that when he succeeded to his family or hereditary titles he was exempted from forfeiture by a special clause in the English Act of Parliament (1st William and Mary); and in Acts afterwards passed in Ireland, in the same reign, to prevent the reversal of various outlawries, &c., it was directed that nothing contained in them should extend to attaint or convict of high treason Nicholas Earl of Carlinford or his brother Francis, &c. (Burke's P.B., &c.).—Schomberg, it is said, exposed himself too much in the battle—anyhow, he had not a sufficiency of defensive armour, and refused, though eagerly desired, to put on his cuirass. His body was interred in St. Patrick's Cathedral, Dublin; and many years afterwards, whilst a grave was being dug, contiguously, his skull was, unknowingly or quite carelessly, disturbed—placed amongst or near some mould thrown upon the surface of the floor, and being left for a while there (so runs the story) it was picked up by a man who was working in the Cathedral and taken away by him. For a while the skull was used by this man to put paint in. Eventually the Cathedral authorities became aware of this, got possession of the skull, and replaced it in the grave out of which it had been so unconcernedly lifted, and then so thoughtlessly or reprehensibly taken away. Macaulay, in his History, says that when Schomberg was raised from the battle ground by his friends " two sabre wounds were on his head and a bullet from a carbine was lodged in his neck." A sketch taken of the skull referred to, before it was replaced, shows that a bullet had penetrated—gone clean through—one side of it.—The body of Dr. Walker (Governor Walker, of Londonderry, who had been made Bishop of that city by William III) was interred, originally, where he fell (at the passage of the Boyne). His widow, some years later, had the remains disinterred, as she believed, and buried on the south side of Castle Caulfield Church, with a suitable inscription; but it is not certain that the bones so disinterred were really Walker's (Dict. of Na. Biog.). Prior to the siege of Londonderry, Walker was the rector of Donaghmore, a parish in co. Tyrone, the church thereof being in the village of Castle Caulfield. The monument at Londonderry—a tall column, surmounted by an effigy of Walker, was erected in 1828.—In 1736 a monument commemorative of the victory won on the Boyne by the forces of William was put up on the north side of the river, on a rock rising from the edge of the water. It is an obelisk of dark-hued limestone, 150 feet high, and bears at its base an inscription relating to the battle and the achievement of William. A bridge now crosses the Boyne close to the monument, and at the spot where the central passage of William's army was effected.

July 2d, 1690.

Very hott. Ye King sent Coll La Mellioniere to summons Drogheda wth a strong body of men and a traine of great gunns. Severall prisoners are brought in here. By one come from Dublin this morning we hear ye enemy have quitted Dublin, and left only some few of ye militia. We stayd all this day att Duleeke, where I saw Mr. French and conferr'd wth him about correspondence and intelligence. I wrote to England.

Ye 3d.—A small shower. We march'd wthin 8 miles of Dublin, whither I went wth a few dragoons, after having secur'd Dubber

THE BOYNE MONUMENT,

At the place where the passage of the soldiers of William III took place.

From a photo by W. Lawrence, Dublin.

and all ye tenants and theyr cattle by one of ye King's life gaurd and some dragoons. I found all freindes att Dublin to admiration well, wthout being massacred, burnt, or stript. I waited on ye Committee att ye castle, and was after wth severall freindes att ye garter tavern, and lay att cousen Corkers that night.

> Dubber was the seat of Sir Richard Bellingham, the diarist's cousin.— Cousin Corker married a daughter of Sir Daniel Bellingham, uncle of the diarist.

Ye 4th.—Very hott. I waited on ye King wth an account of ye stores and provisions yt were in Dublin and 20 miles round. I presented him wth a baskett of cherryes, ye first he eat since he came to ye kingdom. He tooke them wth his own hand very kindly. I return'd to Dubber, and distributed ye peoples cattle to ye right owners and gave them protections. I lay there yt night.

Ye 5th.—Very hott. I came this morning to Dublin, din'd wth my father [father-in-law], wrote severall letters for England. We hear yt K James tooke shipping att Waterford, and yt his whole army were disperst. Our army advanc'd and pitch't theyr camp near Finglas.

> James reached Waterford Harbour early in the morning of July 3rd. Soon afterwards he left, by sea, for Kinsale, and on arriving there he proceeded, in a French frigate, to Brest. He afterwards went to St. Germain-en-Laye (13 miles west of Paris), where he resided in an old royal chateau till his death, on the 6th of September, 1701. In the latter part of 1906 the Paris " Gaulois " remarked that " many Irish soldiers "—adherents of James II— " settled down in Lorraine, and there are Lorraine houses where they [the occupants] still pray for the Stuarts with a fidelity to the memory of the fallen dynasty of which there are very few examples in England even."— Finglas is a parish and post town three miles w. of Dublin.

Ye 6th [Sunday].—A hott but gloomy day. Ye King wth all ye nobillity came to town, and heard Dr. King preach att St. Pattricks. There was great joy att ye King's arrivall, by bonefires, etc. I was att St. Owen's, and in ye afternoon went wth Capt Ponell and Brereton to view ye castle, and from thence we went to ye Garter tavern.

> St. Patrick's, i.e., Dublin Cathedral. Macaulay says (History of England), "Doctor King preached, with all the fervour of a neophyte, on the great deliverance which God had wrought for the Church."

Ye 7th.—Some showers. I went wth Sr Rich B., my father, Handcock, and Capt Frowde to ye camp. We din'd att Dubber. I gott protections for several freindes in West Meath. We have a rumour of a fight wth ye French att sea, but not to our advantage. Here are great feares of some French shipping coming on our coastes to burn our ships. Had a letter from Nabby.

> Sr Rich B. was Sir Richard Bellingham, the diarist's uncle.—"My father" was the diarist's father-in-law, William Handcock, of Twyford.— Capt. Frowde would be the "cousin Frowde" mentioned in the entry for Feb. 15th, 1688-9. He was the Philip Frowde who married Sarah, daughter of Sir Daniel Bellingham, Bt., widow of George Blount.

Ye 8th.—Some showers. I went wth my cousen Corker to ye camp, where he waited on Sr Robt Southwell and was kindly receiv'd. I din'd wth ye Earl of Scarborough. Severall came to see ye camp. Sr R. B. was very drunke. I lay this night att Dubber.

> Sir Robert Southwell was Clerk of the Privy Council of Charles II, Envoy Extraordinary to various Courts afterwards, and principal Secretary of State for Ireland in 1690. He died in 1702. His son Edward, who succeeded him, was principal Secretary for Ireland.—The Earl of Scarborough was Richard, created the first Earl of that name on April 15th, 1690.

Ye 9th.—Much raine. Douglass went wth a strong detachment of about 10,000 towards Athloan. Ye King wth ye rest of ye army encamp'd about Cromlin. We hear of some Protestants being killed about Enniskorthy, in ye county of Wexford, and yt ye town is taken by ye Protestants of it and resolve to hould it out. There are some horse sent to theyr reliefe.

> Cromlin, i.e., Crumlin, is a parish three miles s.w. of the city of Dublin.

1. *Principal Gateway Entrance, Castle Bellingham.*   3. *Castle and Lake (s. view).*
2. *Avenue—view from Castle to Gateway.*   4. *Castlebellingham Village.*

Ye 10th.—Some showers. Rochfort and Pim went to Cromlin to receive ye King's commands. I saw Reny Graham and other prisoners in ye castle. I tooke leave of M. G. Kirke and wrote some letters for England.

Ye 11th.—Some showers. Ye King decamp'd from Crumlin to march towards Munster. Fresh feares of ye French coming to burn our ships. Sr R B, G W, Mr. Maynard, and I went on board ye Ruby and came home late.

Ye 12th.—Very hott. Orders given for my being Sheriffe of Lowth. Waited on ye Lds Comms, gave my security, and was late wth R. Twigg att his chamber in Castle street.

Ye 13th.—Very hott. I tooke out my commission for Sheriffe. Went to St. Patts [Patrick's], where one Burridge preach'd. Din'd att Cous Corkers, and came yt night to Dubber.

Ye 14th.—Severall showers. I call'd att Killroo, Peacockstowne, and Ratoth. Stayed some time att Drogheda. Gave letters to Mounsieur Signalie, ye French Governour, and came home about 9 att night, where I found Luke King.

Home would be at Gernonstowne.

Ye 15th.—Fayr day. I viewd Milltown, Whiterath, Kincoole, and Derver. Came home by Williamstowne, where I agreed for cutting ye corne.

Ye 16th.—Some showers. Mr. Towneley, Tisdall, Fortescue, and Garstin were sworn justices of ye peace and I Sherriffe. A Danish Comissary Generall lay here very sick. I had letters from Nabby, etc. Mr. Sheeres [? Shales] call'd here. Ye Dane was Ld Rosenheim.

Descendants or representatives of the families with whom those who were sworn justices were connected now own property in the county of Louth.

Ye 17th.—Severall showers.   I had my mowing grass and reaping corne.   I struck some fellows who were destroying Neddy Whites corne.   J. White is very ill ; but we hope it will prove only an ague.   One Beaumont, sonne of Major Beaumont, of Ponfrett, was wth me att supper.   He speakes very bigg, and sayes he killd severall men and tooke 2 horses ye day of ye battle.

The Whites would be persons living in the neighbourhood.—Ponfrett is, no doubt, intended for Pomfret, i.e., Pontefract, in Yorkshire.—The battle means that on the Boyne.

Ye 18th.—A fayr day, but windy.   I was att Williamstowne, Maine, and Milestown.   Came home by Linns.   Saw ye net drawn and tooke a salmon.   I mark't my cattle.   Ye men who were wounded att Newry came here.

Ye 19th.—hott weather.   We had a markett.   I sent ye cattle away.   In ye afternoone I went to Lurgan to shoote rabbetts.

Ye 20th.—A fayr day.   Mr. Houghton preach'd.   We had near 60 in our congregation.   Sr Rich Reeves call'd and stay'd some time wth me.   We have no good account from sea.   I had a letter from Nabby.

Sir Rich Reeves, i.e., Ryves, Recorder of Dublin, knighted in 1681.

Ye 21th.—Much raine.   J. White's distemper proves an ague. I tooke upp some money and received some from ye tenants. I was wth some of them att Patt Whites, where ye Miller and Hen. Calan had a great quarrell about Dan.

Ye 22th.—Very much raine.   I gave Patt White a Dose of Rhubarb infus'd in usquebagh.   J. White continues ill.   I bought 20 sheep from Patt Waaste, of Dromleck, for £4.

£4 would be equal to about £12 of present-day money.

CASTLE BELLINGHAM.

Present View—Front Entrance.

Ye 23th.—A dry day. I found ye tear of Wmstowne [Williams-town] gave some meadow. receiv'd newes of Athloan being invested wthin musket shott of ye castle, and summons sent to Waterford. No good account from England. I had a ler [letter] from Jenny.

Tear is probably intended for ter, as a contraction of terrier, which, in a legal sense, means a list or register of lands.

Ye 24th.—A gloomy day. We held a private sessions, where we had a full meeting of Protestants. We heard severall petitions about ye plunderers, and chose high constables for ye severall Baronyes in the county.

Ye 25th.—A hott day. I went to Dunany and adjousted matters wth Mr. Gernon. Call'd att Salterstowne. Brought home 3 of my cattle from Dunany. Att my return I found ye Marchioness of Antrim here, wth whom I din'd. An ensign and some sick men of Cutt's Regiment lay here.

Dunany is a parish in co. Louth, five miles n.e. of Dunleer, its post town. Dunany House, situated in this parish, was the seat of Robert Sibthorp, Esq., the diarist's cousin on the mother's side. About 1804 Dunany and Salterstown were purchased by Sir William Bellingham.—The Marchioness of Antrim was Helena, third daughter of Sir John Burke, Knt., of Derry Maclaghtry, co. Galway. She was the second wife of Alexander, third Earl of Antrim, and Lord Lieutenant of the county of Antrim, who was a keen adherent of James II in the war of the revolution, was charged with high treason, but was afterwards included in the treaty of Limerick, and had his lands, &c., restored.

Ye 26th.—A fayr day. I seized some men who ingratefully stole R. Ling of Dundalkes sword and coate. He and ye Serjeant made them buy theyr theft dearly. All ye lead is cutt in Wmstowne and made upp.

Wmstowne, i.e., Williamstown, is a village three miles s.e. of Dublin. The lead would be taken from buildings, and then melted down and cast into bullets, &c.

Ye 27th.—Very hott. Mr. Nixon gave us a very good sermon. Severall freindes din'd wth me. We receiv'd ye good newes of Waterford and Duncannon being surrendred.

> Mr. Nixon appears to have been the Rev. Adam Nixon, who entered Trinity College, Dublin, July 5th, 1679, aged 17; Scholar, 1682; B.A., 1683; M.A., 1686. He was son of George Nixon, of Granshagh, co. Fermanagh. Having been curate successively of Drumcondra and St. Werburgh's, in Dublin diocese (being curate at the latter to William King, afterwards Archbishop), he obtained on the 15th of September, 1690, the College living of Aghalurcher, diocese of Clogher, became Vicar-General and Chancellor of the Diocese, and was in the Commission of the Peace for co. Fermanagh. The contemporary Betham—Phillips' MS. History of the county—calls him " a man of learning and sound judgment." He married, before 1696, Mary, eldest daughter of Daniel Eccles, of Shannock, co. Fermanagh, High Sheriff for that county, 1675. The Rev. Adam Nixon died intestate, administration being granted on the 8th of March, 1716-17. His grandson, Major-General Sir Eccles Nixon, Madras Army, had a long and adventurous career in India. There is a tradition in the Nixon family that one of that generation was Chaplain to William III. Here we find a Mr. Nixon officiating in the neighbourhood immediately after the Battle of the Boyne.

Ye 28th.—Very hott. I went wth Mr. Tisdell towards Dublin. Din'd att Drogheda, and had ye newes of Douglass rising from Athloan.

Ye 29th.—The King came to Chapple Izzod

> Chapple Izzod, i.e., Chapelizod, is a village about three miles west of Dublin. Its name is said to have been derived from Izod, the daughter of Angus, King of Ireland.

Ye 30th.—Much raine. Great concourse to see ye King.

Ye 31th.—Some raine. I waited on my Lady Bellingham to see ye King.

> Lady Bellingham was Jane, daughter of William Barlow, of Littleborough, in Lancashire, and was the widow of Sir Daniel Bellingham.

August ye 1st.

Some raine. I gave in my petition to ye Comrs [Commissioners]. Ye K[ing] went to ye camp, which is on its march to Limrick.

SIR HENRY BELLINGHAM, BART.,

Present Representative of the Family.

Ye 2d.—Very fayre. We arriv'd before Limrick after beating ye enemy out of all ye feilds and ditches.   I went to Dubber on ye 3d, and on

Ye 4th I went to Sr Rich B : to Raboth.   Nothing materall till ye 10th.   I went to Clontarfe : din'd there, and went to Dubber.

No entries between the 4th and the 11th.

Ye 11th.—I went to cousen Swans, and stay'd most of ye day. This night about 12 a clock Sarsfield wth a party of horse seized our great guns att Cullen, and spoyld our boates ; but 6 of 8 guns were againe recover'd.   Women and children kill'd by ye enemy.

Cousin Swan was Jane, daughter of Sir Daniel Bellingham, and had married Edward Swan, of Killrisk, co. Dublin.—Sarsfield was an Irish Jacobite general.   Some particulars about him are given in a previous note (p. 44).—Cullen is a parish and village, five miles n.w. of the town of Tipperary, and on the road from that place to Limerick.

No entries between the 11th and the 17th.

Ye 17th.—Still fayr weather. We opened ye trenches this night, and beat ye enemy out of several forts and sconces, and in one fort we kill'd 80 ; Kirke giving them the same quarter wch they gave our waggoners.

Sconces—works for defence, hut-like places for protection.

Ye 18th.—This night by mistake our men fell foul on each other, and fir'd and kill'd about 20. Ye enemy made a sally, but were repulls'd wth considerable loss.

Ye 19th.—Our men reliev'd theyr guards about 4 in ye afternoone, to prevent ye inconvenience of last night's mistake, occasioned by ye darkness of ye night.

Ye 20th.—In ye morning we batter'd ye remaining fort ye enemy were possess't of wthout [i.e., outside] theyr counterscarp. About 2 in ye afternoon we storm'd it wth a detachment of Grenadiers, who wthin halfe an houre tooke it, putting 150 to the sword, sparing only theyr Capt Barrett, by ye Ks [King's] order. About 5 ye enemy made a vigorous sally wth ye best of theyr force, both horse and foote, and after near an houre's dispute were beaten into ye town, leaving 500 dead in ye place.

No entry for the 21st.

Ye 22th.—About 5 this morning ye enemy made another sally ; but theyr last loss and defeat made them more wary, and retir'd in less than a quarter of an hour wth some loss.

No entries between the 22nd and the 27th.

Ye 27th.—This day ye King order'd counterscarp to be storm'd, which our men did wth great bravery, and beat ye enemy into ye town, after whom our men, pursuing too farr, severall both officers and soldiers were kill'd, by the springing up of severall mines, and ye rest forc'd to retire. This day I returned home.

The fighting referred to was at Limerick.—Home, i.e., Gernonstown.

No entry for the 28th.

Ye 29th.—The King designed to storme ye town [Limerick] this day ; but, the raines falling so heavily these 2 dayes past and the trenches so full of water, it was thought fitter to raise ye seige. This day Mr. Fowkes dy'd.

Ye 30th.—Mr. Fowkes was buryd att Ardee. This morning our army decamp'd from before Limrick, and ye King went to Waterford, in order to embarque for England.

BELLINGHAM MEMORIAL CRUCIFIX,

At Castlebellingham.

Sbr ye 2d.   [No entry for the 1st.]

The Comns [Commissioners] of array and gentlemen of ye county mett att Ardee, appointed officers and men for ye militia, and comtted several Papists for not bringing [in] theyr armes according to ye Proclamation.

Ye 3d.—This day ye Comns of array mett againe at Gernons-towne and settled ye price of ye armes and signed warrants for ye apprehending severall Papists.

No entry for the 4th.

Ye 5th.—This day ye Comrs of array mett att Dunleere and disposed of severall horses which were taken upp from Papists. About 3 this afternoon ye King tooke shipping att Duncannon fort for England.

No entry for the 6th.

Ye 7th.—Much raine fallen this weeke past. Randall Moore dyed this morning.

Randall Moore was the fourth son of Charles, second Viscount Drogheda. He lived at Ardee, in co. Louth, and was attainted by King James' Parliament in 1689.

Ye 8th.—I loaded my hay for Drogheda.

Ye 9th.—We buryd Randall Moore, att Drogheda, in ye tomb.

The tomb was in St. Peter's Church, Drogheda, the burial place of the Moore family.

Ye 10th.—High wind and raine. I return'd from Drogheda.

Ye 11th.—Much raine. My troop mett, but ill arm'd and mounted. They show great zeal for ye service. I divided ye horses.

Ye 12th.—Some raine.   A party of soldiers under ye command of one Ensigne Jeff, of Coll Brewers Regiment, pressed all ye horses on our road.   I sent a party after them, who brought them back, but upon theyr submission dismissd them.

(END OF THE DIARY).

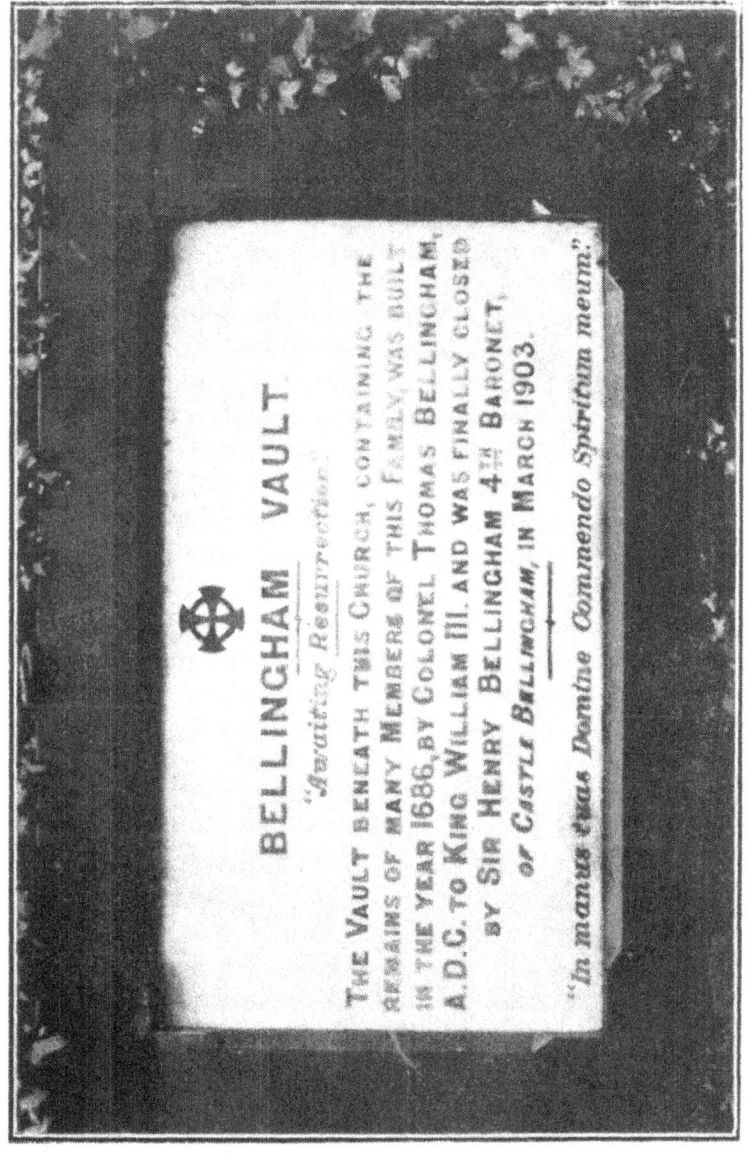

BELLINGHAM BURIAL VAULT.

Copy of Tablet at the Burial Place of Colonel Bellingham, his parents, &c.

This vault, made by the Colonel, is under the Protestant Episcopal Church in the village of Gernonstown, now called Castlebellingham.

PEDIGREE TABLES.

Descent of the Diarist as wrongly given, by the Herald Francis Townsend, in 1796.

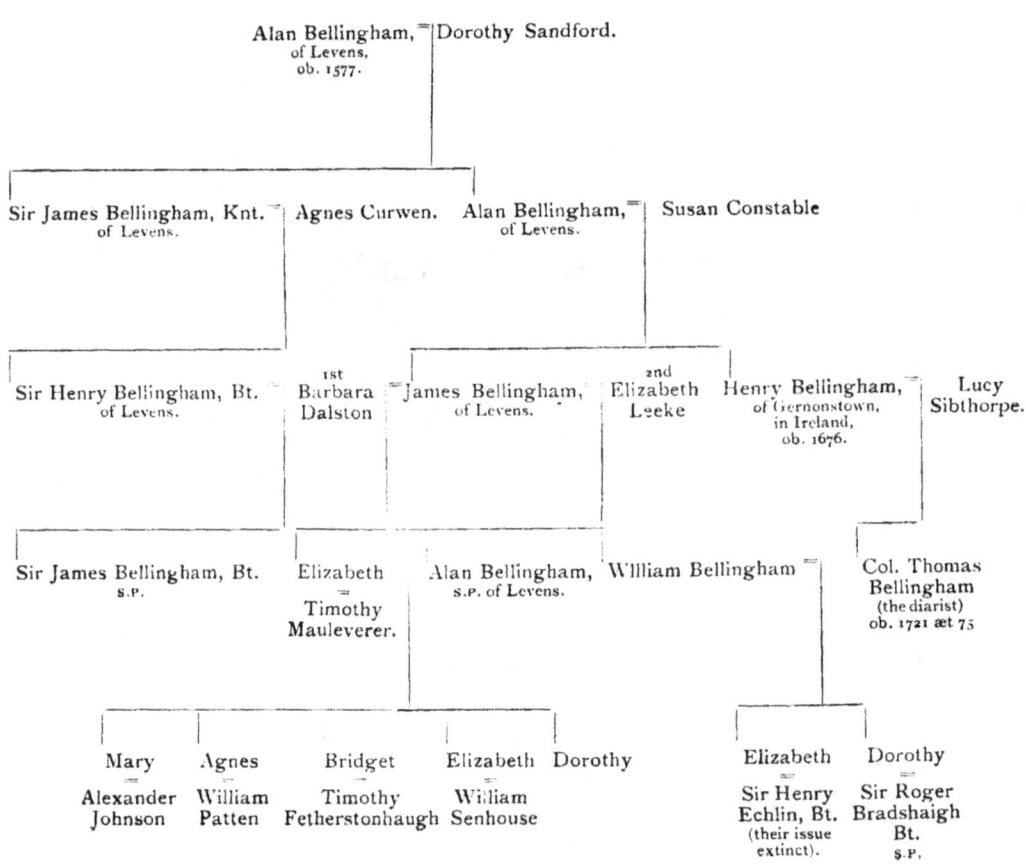

Descent of the Diarist as rightly given.

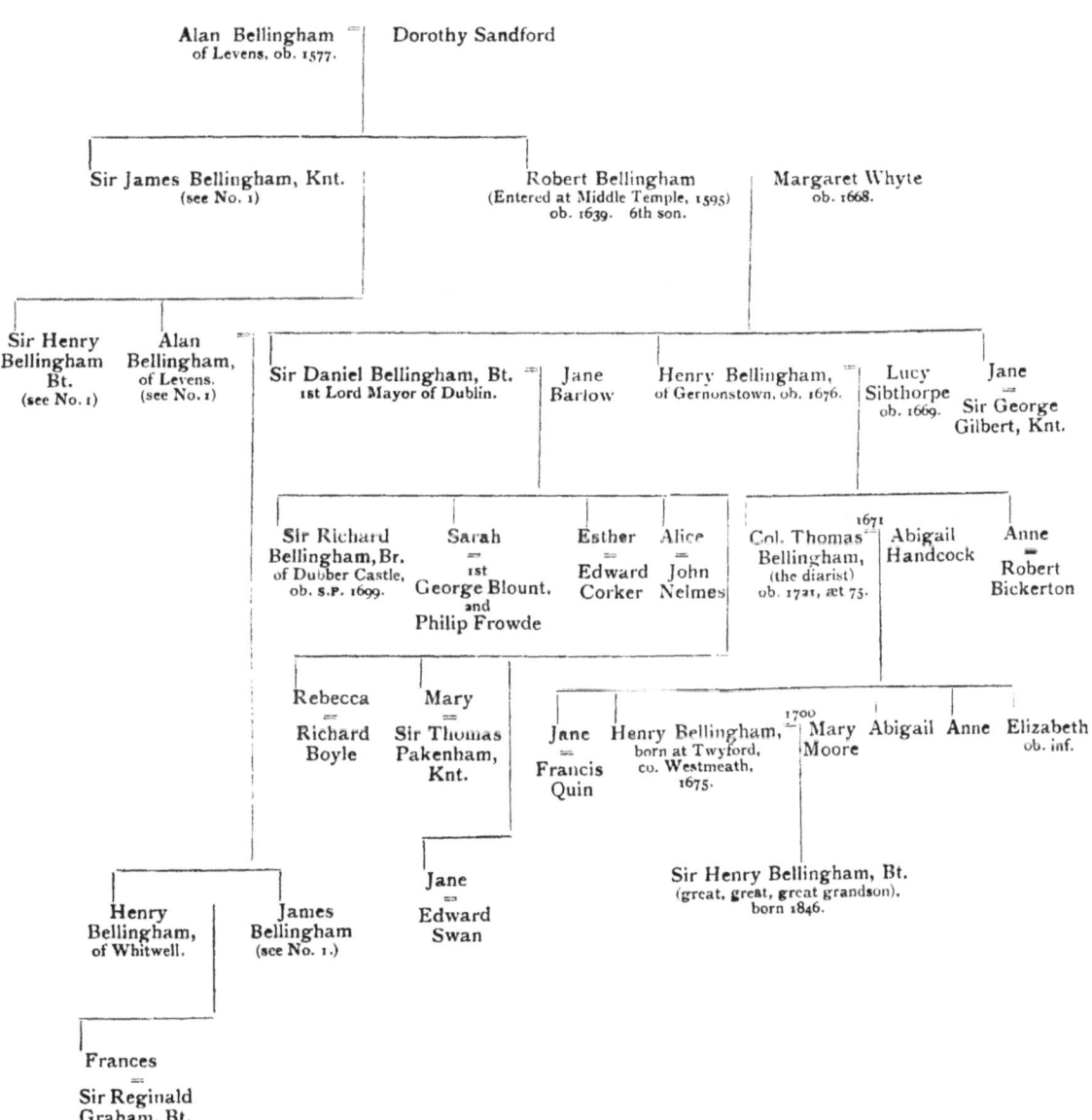

Alan Bellingham = Dorothy Sandford
of Levens, ob. 1577.

Sir James Bellingham, Knt.   Robert Bellingham   Margaret Whyte
(see No. 1)   (Entered at Middle Temple, 1595)   ob. 1668.
ob. 1639. 6th son.

Sir Henry   Alan   Sir Daniel Bellingham, Bt.   Jane   Henry Bellingham,   Lucy   Jane
Bellingham   Bellingham,   1st Lord Mayor of Dublin.   Barlow   of Gernonstown, ob. 1676.   Sibthorpe   =
Bt.   of Levens.   ob. 1669.   Sir George
(see No. 1)   (see No. 1)   Gilbert, Knt.

Sir Richard   Sarah   Esther   Alice   1671   Abigail   Anne
Bellingham, Br.   =   =   =   Col. Thomas =   Handcock   =
of Dubber Castle,   1st   Edward   John   Bellingham,   Robert
ob. s.p. 1699.   George Blount.   Corker   Nelmes   (the diarist)   Bickerton
2nd   ob. 1721, æt 75.
Philip Frowde

Rebecca   Mary   Jane   Henry Bellingham,   1700 Mary   Abigail   Anne   Elizabeth
=   =   =   born at Twyford,   Moore   ob. inf.
Richard   Sir Thomas   Francis   co. Westmeath,
Boyle   Pakenham,   Quin   1675.
Knt.

Jane   Sir Henry Bellingham, Bt.
=   (great, great, great grandson),
Edward   born 1846.
Swan

Henry   James
Bellingham,   Bellingham
of Whitwell.   (see No. 1.)

Frances
=
Sir Reginald
Graham, Bt.

ERRATA, &c.

Page 29, second note, Enlgand should be England.

Page 107, bottom note.—Rigby was presumably a grandson, not a son, of Mr. Edward Rigby who was M.P. for Preston from 1661 to 1681.

Pages xviii and xix, introduction, Townshend should be Townsend.

Cousin Frowde, mentioned on pp. 12, 51, 52, &c., was Philip Frowde, Postmaster General under James II, and the son of Sir Philip Frowde, of Kent, who was knighted on March 10th, 1664-65.

INDEX.

158 INDEX.

PRESTON : PRINTED BY GEO. TOULMIN AND SONS, 127, FISHERGATE.